A TIME

o f

DEPARTING

A TIME
of
DEPARTING

How a universal spirituality
Is changing the face of Christianity

Ray Yungen

Lighthouse Trails Publishing Company
Silverton, Oregon, U.S.A.

A TIME OF DEPARTING

©2002 by Ray Yungen
First Edition
Third Printing

Published by
Lighthouse Trails Publishing Company
P.O. Box 958
Silverton, Oregon 97381
editor@lighthousetrails.com
www.lighthousetrails.com

DISCLAIMER

Author and Publisher have used their best efforts in making this book, including all endnotes and quotes, as accurate as possible. In the event that any inaccuracy occur, this is unintentional, and we apologize for such oversights.

It is not the intent of the Author or Publisher to imply any sort of sinister motives or deliberate attempt to mislead or deceive by any of the individuals or organizations critiqued in this book. We believe these people are honest, sincere persons of good will.

Also when the term occult/occultism is used in this book, it is not a referral to the often held portrayal of Satanism but rather refers to the hidden perceptions of the mystical realm (i.e., God-in-all worldview).

International Standard Book Number
0-9721512-0-6
Library of Congress Catalogue Card Number
2002108357

Note: *A Time of Departing* is included with glossary, index and endnotes for the convenience of the serious Bible student. Bulk copies (10 or more) of this book are available at discount prices.

Printed in the United States of America

To Mother and Dad
Who Did So Much For Me

Acknowledgments

Thank you to all of the wonderful brothers and sisters in our Lord who stood beside me, aided me and encouraged me in the making of this book. You know who you are and I am forever indebted. May God bless you for your steadfastness.

What Others Are Saying About *A Time of Departing*

Is contemplative prayer really a vehicle to a closer walk with God? *A Time of Departing* documents clearly that far from being such a vehicle, contemplative prayer is more akin to a Trojan Horse. You may be very surprised to read of who the prime pawns are in this spiritually dangerous deception.

CECIL ANDREWS

TAKE HEED MINISTRIES - NORTHERN IRELAND
www.takeheed.net.

The church is under subtle attack. Pantheistic theology and occult practices have become a serious danger to the purity of the true gospel of Jesus Christ. Ray Yungen is a Watchman sounding the alarm.

PHILLIP ARNN

SENIOR RESEARCHER, WATCHMAN FELLOWSHIP, INC.
www.watchman.org

Ray Yungen exposes, in a clear and documented manner, both Catholic and Evangelical mysticism, which has affected mankind in its core beliefs and values. I highly recommend this book to understand a massive undetected plague facing us in our day.

RICHARD BENNETT

FORMER CATHOLIC PRIEST, NOW EVANGELIST - BEREAN BEACON
www.bereanbeacon.org

Explains the implications of Contemplative Spirituality; prayer is replaced by unbiblical mystical techniques, Christian spirituality is replaced by an unscerning mysticism, and reliance on the Bible to shape our image of God is replaced by contemplative experience. *A* must read.

JOHN CADDOCK

AUTHOR OF *WHAT IS CONTEMPLATIVE SPIRITUALITY AND WHY IS IT SO DANGEROUS* -
JOURNAL OF THE GRACE EVANGELICAL SOCIETY, AUTUMN 1997

After reading *A Time of Departing* one can only come to the conclusion that contemplative prayer is one of the introductory gateways into Eastern mysticism. While popular theologians are Christianizing Eastern mysticism, the reality is Christianity is being spiritualized into this realm.

GREG DESVOIGNES

CHRISTIAN RESEARCH MINISTRIES
www.crmspokane.org

Contemplative prayer is an Eastern style meditation dressed up in Christian clothing. Unfortunately, the Christian community is caught unaware. Mr. Yungen's book alerts its readers that there is a growing movement within the church that must be stopped.

BRIAN FLYNN

DIRECTOR - NOW AGE SEMINARS
www.thenowage.org

Gives keen insights into the subtle attacks on the gospel by agents of the master deceiver. Provides the discernment that the church needs in these days of widespread deception. Will help keep the reader's heart from being led astray from its pure devotion to Jesus Christ.

EVANGELIST MIKE GENDRON

DIRECTOR, PROCLAIMING THE GOSPEL
www.pro-gospel.org

A very enlightening report on some of the dangers creeping into the church today.

PASTOR ALLAN HANSEN

FOUNDER CHRISTIAN RENEWAL CENTER - OREGON
www.christianrenewalcenter.org

Brings attention to an important late 20th and early 21st century mysticism which is infiltrating Christianity ... Those involved in contemplative prayer have departed from the biblical teaching on prayer and have incorporated Eastern religious elements that are directly in conflict with Scripture.

DR. WAYNE HOUSE

DISTINGUISHED PROFESSOR OF BIBLICAL AND THEOLOGICAL STUDIES
OREGON THEOLOGICAL SEMINARY
www.oregontheologicalseminary.org

A well researched, valuable book ... a solid critique of meditative and contemplative *prayer* and should alert others who may not be aware of the dangers. Good insight into how universal this *silence* for guidance and *light* can become—Ray has hit the nail right on the head!

WENDY HOWARD

DESPATCH MAGAZINE - AUSTRALIA
www.despatch.cth.com.au/Main/

[*A Time of Departing*] is excellent. It goes to the heart of pagan spirituality and courageously asks how this false approach is deeply affecting the evangelical church ... I recommend this book without hesitation.

PETER JONES
AUTHOR OF PAGANS IN THE PEWS
www.spirit-wars.com

A vital resource for understanding our times, for recognizing deception and for resisting today's most enticing distortions of truth. I recommend this book to all.

BERIT KJOS
KJOS MINISTRIES
www.crossroad.to

This book fills a great need in our present day. ...the scriptures quoted give authenticity to the points Ray makes. Deserves wide recognition.

BERNIE KOERSELMAN
BEREAN PUBLISHERS
www.bereanpublishers.com

Many who call themselves Christians participate in and promote many of the techniques used by New Agers including contemplative or centering prayer. It is extremely important that this message gets out to the Christian community.

PASTOR MICHAEL KOLE
JESUS FELLOWSHIP - SAN DIEGO
FORMER NEW AGER FOR 20 YEARS

Mr. Ray Yungen has brought out the core of what the agenda of the New Age mystic is all about —to enter the Christian Church. Excellent book and a must read for every Christian!

DR. JIMMY LOWERY
J.E.LOWERY MINISTRIES
www.jelm.net

Sadly, many pastors are oblivious to the unbiblical concepts promoted within their churches. *A Time of Departing* clearly shows how [New Age] spiritual deception is being introduced into the church. A must read for all pastors and teachers who want to protect their churchs from deception.

KEITH MACGREGOR
MACGREGOR MINISTRIES - B.C. CANADA
www.macgregorministries.org

As a former professional astrologer and New Age practitioner of Hindu and Buddhist meditation, I recognize in the contemplative prayer movement many of the same techniques and views I once had. This book is crucial for understanding the infiltration of Eastern views in the Church.

MARCIA MONTENEGRO
CANA (CHRISTIAN ANSWERS FOR THE NEW AGE)
http://cana.userworld.com

A Time of Departing opens a new door of knowledge to those earnestly contending for the faith. There is a New Religion in town and it is called New Age, as amply exposed in this book by Mr. Yungen.

ANDY NECKAR
CHRISTIAN NEWS AND VIEWS
http://cnview.com

Well written, researched and documented. Provides a sobering overview of how far the Christian church has been influenced by the deception of the New Age movement.

ROGER OAKLAND
UNDERSTAND THE TIMES
www.understandthetimes.org

Ray Yungen makes us aware that the New Age movement has not faded into oblivion but has found a new avenue of reception in the church ... documents how mysticism is being accepted and practiced as prayer. A great resource as well as a warning for discerning Christians.

MIKE OPPENHEIMER
DIRECTOR, LET US REASON MINISTRIES
www.letusreason.org

Thank you Ray for again sounding the alarm about a very real danger to the church. A wake-up call to all pastors, leaders, and Christians eveywhere who care about the integrity of the "faith delivered to us once and for all."

PASTOR BILL RANDLES
MIDNIGHT HERALD
http://awake-ministries.org

Ray Yungen has sounded a wake up call for all evangelical Christians. His research and documentation clearly reveal that New Age mysticism is not only alive but growing and infiltrating orthodox Christianity. Makes clear we either respond to heresy or become assimilated by it.

R. J. ROONEY, JR., M. DIV

FOUNDER AND AUTHOR OF FORTHEFAITH.COM AND U.M. PASTOR

A very important book. Panentheism has invaded the churches in a variety of ways already, but the introduction of contemplative prayer is sure to be a final nail to the coffin. Ray does a good job of research and has applied excellent authorship and readability to *A Time of Departing*.

SANDY SIMPSON

DECEPTION IN THE CHURCH
www.deceptioninthechurch.com

I am recommending the book to all those connected to our ministry and totally endorse its contents. In these last days of "deception" it is crucial that our people be informed of this error."

PASTOR KEN SUMRALL

THE CHURCH FOUNDATIONAL NETWORK
www.churchfoundationalnetwork.com

Author removes the covers from much that passes for Christian teaching and exposes it as a dangerous deception. If you are seeking guidance on knowing truth from error, *A Time of Departing* will not disappoint you!

TRICIA TILLIN

BANNER MINISTRIES - UK
www.banner.org.uk

I especially appreciate Yungen's warnings about the influence of mysticism on contemporary evangelical spirituality.

DR. DONALD S. WHITNEY

ASSOCIATE PROFESSOR OF SPIRITUAL FORMATION
MIDWESTERN BAPTIST THEOLOGICAL SEMINARY
www.spiritualdisciplines.org

A great tool to create an awareness in young people ...
Author points out that Jesus has become a commodity used in
almost all belief systems to make them believable. The book
is an important addition to educate people.

GEORGE AND RITA WILLIAMS

CEPHAS MINISTRY INC. - ZEPHYRHILLS, FLORIDA

www.cephasministry.com

Reminds us that New Age philosophy has infiltrated a great deal
of literature dealing with *spirituality* ...the reader will be warned
of false teachers and of those within the evangelical camp who
have been so influenced. I will have my students study this work.

ROBERT W. WRIGHT, PH.D

PROFESSOR OF WORLD RELIGIONS AND CULTS

WESTERN BAPTIST COLLEGE, SALEM, OREGON

www.wbc.edu

For the first three centuries of Church history Christians out
thought and out lived their pagan counterparts and influenced
civilization. For the last 150 years the pagan culture has influenced
the Church .... *A Time of Departing* is an excellent primer in
assisting believers who are serious about defending the faith.

L.L. (DON) VEINOT JR., PRESIDENT

MIDWEST CHRISTIAN OUTREACH, INC.

www.midwestoutreach.org

New Age wolves are feasting on the flock again, and their
latest sheep costumes are state of the art. Any Christian leader
who takes his flock protection duty seriously needs to read
A Time of Departing—A vital book.

MARK VRANKOVICH

DIRECTOR OF CULTWATCH INC. - NEW ZEALAND

www.cultwatch.com

CONTENTS

FOREWORD

I once had the opportunity to pilot a KC-135R Airforce simulator. The actual plane is a huge tanker that refuels fighter jets while in the air. A friend of mine knew a major in the Air Force who guided us through this incredible experience. Jumping into the cockpit of such technology was a bit overwhelming compared to the physics of my Toyota 4x4. Yet with all the complexities of this aircraft, I was surprised how easily the plane lifted off. However, I was about to learn the true test of my piloting skills was going to be with the landing. After my erratic flight over the landscape, I was all over the sky while attempting to line up with the runway. Even though I had all the instruments and even an expert next to me, I eventually crashed. Without question, my intentions were noble and good; the problem was I lacked the knowledge and discernment to land the plane safely.

A Time of Departing is about *spiritual* pilots whose desired destination may be noble and good, but their actual destination is a departure from the saving faith of Christ's work on the Cross and a departure from Biblical truth that proclaims: "He who has the Son has life; he who does not have the Son of God does not have life" (I John 5:12).

These religious navigators offer both a practical and mystical spirituality that leads to euphoric experiences. The resulting popular spirituality claims to possess an enlightenment that all religions need. Its roots are found in Eastern mystical religions and in New Age Western thought. This mystical spirituality is not that difficult to identify—for it has now saturated Western civilization and has crossed the barriers of the Christian church at an astonishing rate. By using Eastern mystical techniques such as the repetition of words (mantras) and the emptying of the mind, professing Christians are testifying to powerful experiences in the spiritual realms. In Christian circles these techniques are being called: the silence, breath prayer, centering prayer, or contemplative prayer. Through these mystical prayer practices the church today has opened its door to a subtle abandonment of the gospel. The late Francis Schaeffer identified the coming of this abandonment in his landmark book, *The God Who Is There:*

> [I]n almost all forms of the new mysticism there is a growing acceptance of the ideas of pantheism [everything is God]. The West and the East are coming together, and these pantheistic concepts are one of the strongest elements in the semantic mysticism of which we are speaking.[1]

Like two rivers merging together, Eastern and Western religious thought are joining together, thus gaining momentum towards a one world religion in which all paths lead to God. A person who understands the unfolding of this new paradigm is Ray Yungen. Ray has devoted most of his adult life to the research of religious movements. For over 20 years Ray has brilliantly demonstrated his expertise in New Ageism and Eastern religions. He not only identifies their belief systems but reveals how their universal ideologies are penetrating our schools, medical field, business, politics, and the church. His first book, *For Many Shall Come in My Name*, unveiled how mainstream America is accepting the teaching of *ancient wisdom.* Now, in this book, *A Time of Departing,* Ray reveals how Christianity has opened its door to a blending of the gospel of Jesus Christ with mystical pantheistic thoughts.

But please take note. Ray is not a conspiracy theorist nor is he an alarmist. Rather, Ray works from painstaking research and Biblical exegesis that helps his readers understand the dangers he is attempting to expose. Ray is devoted to Jesus Christ, and he loves people. Nonetheless, he is also compelled to share the information that his research has unveiled. It is his hope that people will turn from false spirituality taught by man and turn fully to the Word of God and their one and only hope—Jesus Christ.

We now live in a time where Biblical discernment is imperative. Ray has exposed false teaching with sound doctrine and with gracious discernment.

Today, as in all of Christian history, there are brilliant minds leading the church. Nevertheless, we should take heed to the words of a wise pastor of the 17th century when he said: "It is a known fact, the grossest heresies have bred in the finest minds."[2]

May God give grace and wisdom to everyone who reads this book and considers the evidence revealed in *A Time of Departing*. Those who are piloting the church today need tremendous discernment—for there is just one runway that lands us safely to eternal life, and the width of this runway is only as wide as the Cross.

It is with great gratitude and a deepened humility that I have had the opportunity to work with Ray and introduce you to this book. As you read it and share its message with others, I pray you will "Let the word of Christ dwell in you richly as you teach and admonish one another with all wisdom ..." (Colossians 3:16).

Ron Comer, Pastor
Eastside Christian Fellowship
Salem, Oregon

1

The Invisible Denomination

Now the Spirit expressly says that in latter times some will depart from the faith, giving heed to deceiving spirits and doctrines of demons.

(I Timothy 4:1)

In the decade of the 1980s the term *New Age movement* inspired a sense of dread in many conservative Christians. This fear stemmed from the conviction that something evil and sinister surrounded this movement and that ominous clouds were on the spiritual horizon. In the '90s this backlash largely subsided, and most Christians forgot about or ignored what seemed so threatening a few years earlier.

But this movement has *not* gone away. In fact, it is very much with us and in ways that may surprise many Christians. By the time the new millennium arrived, the New Age had so quietly soaked into our Western culture that many Christians today are literally acclimated and accepting of Gnostic and Eastern spirituality. *A Time of Departi*ng unveils this new spiritual paradigm and reveals the many different manifestations it has taken.

If you are a person who believes we have reached the "latter times" or are right on the threshold, then I Timothy 4:1 should be of keen interest to you. Why? Because if we are indeed in those times, some evidence of this abandonment should be around somewhere. Furthermore, what kind of Christian would be so vulnerable and susceptible to "deceiving spirits?" The nominal Christian? The carnal Christian? You might be surprised at the answer.

How can one recognize Christian teaching that has not been endorsed by Jesus Christ or His apostles? *A Time of Departing* will help the followers of Jesus (His church) recognize the subtle teachings of deceiving spirits—spirits that are ushering in a rethinking of Christianity through teachings that can lead many into a spirituality that may cause them to abandon the faith. This new spirituality, even now, is manifesting itself within some of our strongest evangelical churches.

This book is not just another attempt to explain the New Age, but rather, an alert to the church of how and through whom New Age thinking is currently creeping into our pulpits, Sunday school classrooms, prayer groups and Bible studies. It is a critical time to heed the warning of the apostle John: "Beloved, do not believe every spirit, but test the spirits, whether they are of God; because many false prophets have gone out into the world" (I John 4:1).

In order to discern the spirits, let us first examine the magnitude and influence the New Age has in current society and define what this movement really involves.

The Scope of the New Age

New Age pundit David Spangler wrote that in 1965, concerning the movement he had embraced: "There weren't many places where such a vision was being taken seriously or even considered."[1] In 1992, two and a half decades later, secular journalist Michael D. Antonio, speaking of the same movement, discovered quite a remarkable change. He revealed:

> [S]ociologists at the University of California at Santa Barbara estimate that as many as 12 million Americans could be considered active participants and another 30 million are avidly interested … New Agers would constitute the third largest religious denomination in America.[2]

By 2002, Bradley University Religious Studies professor Robert C. Fuller not only verified these findings but actually increased the figures to an astounding 20 percent of Americans (forty million people) who now embrace the New Age movement.[3] We are no longer talking about the minuscule smattering of spiritual adventurers in 1965 Spangler referred to. Something significant has indeed occurred!

There are those who might be skeptical of the validity of these statistics. Some may feel they are exaggerated and outlandish—and with good reason. If the New Age is so pervasive, why aren't the outer trappings of it apparent on every street? This is an essential question. One dependable way of validating the size of a movement is through the law of the market. Supply, as a rule, corresponds with demand. Business people, financially, live or die by the rule of supply and demand. A continual, large supply of any commodity indicates a large demand; a small supply reflects little demand. It's as simple as that.

The demand for New Age teachings speaks clearly from the law of the market. For example, the number of shelves devoted to New Age spirituality at any sizable national chain bookstore is easily 50-80 shelves. In many cases, the New Age material is rivaling or even outstripping the number of shelves containing Christian books. And in some stores, the New Age sections equal or surpass the sports section.

Further, a number of recent New Age books have sold so well they have become what are called *cultural phenomena*. Books such as *Simple Abundance, The Celestine Prophecy* (eight million copies sold), *Conversations With God* (three million sold) and *The Seven Spiritual Laws of Success* have impacted literally tens of millions of people. The last title by Deepak Chopra (a New Age guru popular with celebrities) was Barnes and Noble's top-selling book for 1996.[4]

New Age healing practices have proliferated to a staggering degree. One such method known as *Reiki* now claims more than 500,000 practitioners in the United States alone.[5] This number is larger than those serving in the U.S. Army! Fifteen years ago there were only several thousand Reiki channelers. Another practice,

Therapeutic Touch, like Reiki, is based on the occult *chakra* system. According to ABC News, Therapeutic Touch has been performed on millions of Americans.

One magazine, *Common Boundary*, which devoted itself to New Age spirituality in the field of counseling and psychotherapy, disclosed in 1994 that its press run had reached 30,000 copies bimonthly.[6] Since the magazine's readers were primarily professionals in these fields it shows the scope of New Age impact in this very influential area. The popular magazine, *TV Guide*, gave credence to the respectability of the New Age viewpoint by including four New Agers in a ten-person list of people it considered as the nation's "prominent spiritual thinkers."[7]

Exactly how did the New Age grow from practically nothing to what it is now in just 30 years? Moreover, why does its outer structure seem so invisible? Why do so many people still think it was just a fad in the '80s and is now history? The answers to these questions provide a disturbing glimpse into one of the most ingenious and skillful grassroots religious engineering efforts in human history.

Why Do They Call it New Age?

The *Aquarian Age* or New Age is supposed to signify that the human race is now entering a golden age. Many occultists have long heralded the Aquarian Age as a time period that would be significant to humanity. That is why one writer stated, "A basic knowledge of astrological ages is of enormous importance in occult work."[8]

The Age of Aquarius is when we are all supposed to realize that *man is God*. As one advocate put it: "A major theme of Aquarius is that *God is within*. The goal of the Age of Aquarius is to bring this idea into meaningful reality" (emphasis mine).[9] Before we can understand how this goal is being pursued, we must first define New Age spirituality. This definition is not as simple as you might think—as one writer pointed out: "It's not so much what New Agers believe that sets them apart from other movements ... but rather how they come by their beliefs ..."[10]

Many Christian writers use such terms as *pantheism* or *monism* in an attempt to explain what New Agers believe; however, these mere words are rather limiting in conveying the total picture. The best explanation I have encountered is from a book entitled *The Mission of Mysticism*. It states:

> Occultism [New Ageism] is defined as the science of mystical evolution; it is the employment of the hidden (i.e., occult) mystical faculties of man to discern the hidden reality of nature; i.e., to see God as the *all in all*" (emphasis mine).[11]

These mystical faculties are the distinguishing mark of the New Age movement—a mystical perception rather than simple belief or faith. An anti-cult Christian writer once described the New Age movement as *a system of thought* when, in fact, it is more aptly defined as a system of *non*-thought. Meditation teacher Ann Wise explained this by stating:

> A man came to see me once saying that he had meditated for an hour a day every day for twelve years. Although he enjoyed the time he spent sitting, he felt he was missing something. From talking to other meditators, he felt that he must have been doing something wrong because he had none of the experiences that he had heard others describe. I measured his brainwaves while he was "meditating" and discovered that he had spent those twelve years simply thinking![12]

This is why New Age style meditation is commonly referred to as *the silence*. This is not silence as being in a quiet place but the silence as in an inner silence or an empty mind that opens up the mystical faculties. "The enemy of meditation is the mind," wrote one New Age teacher.[13]

What Exactly is Meditation?

The meditation most of us are familiar with involves a deep, continuous thinking about something. But New Age meditation does just the opposite. It involves ridding oneself of all thoughts in order to *still* the mind by putting it in the equivalent of pause or neutral. A comparison would be that of turning a fast-moving stream into a still pond. When meditation is employed by damming the free flow of thinking, it holds back active thought and causes a shift in consciousness. This condition is not to be confused with daydreaming, where the mind dwells on a subject. New Age meditation works as a holding mechanism until the mind becomes thoughtless, empty and silent.

The two most common methods used to induce this thoughtless state are *breathing* exercises, where attention is focused on the breath, and a *mantra*, which is a repeated word or phrase. The basic process is to focus and maintain concentration without thinking about what you are focusing on. Repetition on the focused object is what triggers the blank mind.

Since mantras are central to New Age meditation, it is important to understand a proper definition of the word. The translation from Sanskrit is *man*, meaning to "think", and *tra*, meaning "to be liberated from."[14] Thus, the word literally means *to escape from thought*. By repeating the mantra, either out loud or silently, the word or phrase begins to lose any meaning it once had. The conscious thinking process is gradually tuned out until an altered state of consciousness is achieved.

But this silence is not the final objective; its attainment is only a means to an end. What that end entails was aptly described by English artist Vanora Goodhart after she embarked on the practice of zen meditation. She recounted:

> [A] light began seeping through my closed eyelids, bright and gentle at first, but growing more and more intense ... there was a great power and strength in this Light ... I felt I was being drawn upwards and in a great and wonderful rush of power that rose even-

tually to a crescendo and bathed me through and
through with glorious burning, embracing Light.[15]

Such dynamic experiences as this are what New Age mysticism is really all about—not just believing in some doctrine or a
faith that is supported by some creed but rather a close personal
contact with a powerful *Presence*. The renowned occultist Dion
Fortune acknowledged: "shifting the consciousness is the key to
all occult training."[16] In other words, meditation is the gateway to
the "light" Goodhart experienced.

The ultimate objective of the meditation effort lies in the concept called the *higher self*. This is thought to be the part of the
individual linked to the divine essence of the Universe, the God
part of man. The goal is to become attuned with the higher self,
thus facilitating the higher self's emergence into the physical realm
bringing the practitioner under the guidance and direction of *God*.
This connection is referred to in New Age circles as: a*wakening,
transformation, enlightenment, self-realization, cosmic consciousness and
superconsciousness*. This is also why an interchangeable term for New
Age is *metaphysics*. Metaphysics means that which is beyond the
physical realm (the unseen realm) and being intimately connected
to those powers not perceived by the normal five senses.

The Impact of Practical Mystics vs. Cults

Evangelical scholar David L. Smith correctly assessed the powerful, yet subtle, impact New Age spirituality was having on society
when he observed:

> Not since Gnosticism at the dawn of the Christian
> era has there arisen a philosophy as pervasive and
> threatening to orthodox Christianity as the New Age
> movement ... It would be difficult to find any area
> of life, which has not been touched or redirected to
> some degree by the concepts of this movement.[17]

Smith recognized that, rather than just a small segment, the general social fabric of society is being impacted. The New Age movement has clearly evolved well past the subculture stage into something much more dynamic and influential. This stunning change has been brought about by the rise of a new breed of mystic—one that presents mysticism as a complement to secular goals and one that is adept at surmounting the public's natural impulse to reject the strange and unfamiliar. Some examples of this are:

A prominent, influential speaker and seminar leader, Brian Tracy, promotes the use of the "superconscious mind" (which is another term for the higher self), "to improve productivity, performance and output" in the corporate world.[18]

An article in one major Pacific Northwest newspaper features a large color picture of a local university professor in a classic zen Buddhist meditation pose. He has not joined the Buddhist religion but is trying to reverse his heart condition through Eastern meditation.[19]

A popular morning talk show entices viewers with the promise of "how to get along with your spouse." The show then features popular New Age author Wayne Dyer exhorting viewers to "go into the silence for guidance" when they get angry with their mate.[20]

These are just a few examples of what could be called *secular mysticism* or generic mysticism, meditation practiced not for religious reasons but as a tool to improve life. Many Christians have a difficult time comprehending this concept. They have been trained to think in terms of cults such as the Mormons (Church of Jesus Christ of Latter Day Saints) or the Watchtower Society (Jehovah's Witnesses). But these groups are rather limited in their impact because, even if they become sizable, they still remain only islands in society. The advantage practical mystics have is that they only have to piggyback a seemingly benevolent meditation method onto whatever programs they are promoting—they do not have to proselytize people to a dogma, only a practice.

New Age publisher Jeremy Tarcher spoke of this challenge in an interview. Speaking of practical mystics he explained: "They have to learn to present their perceptions in appropriate language and actions that don't arouse fear or resistance."[21]

Because of their success at this effort, one writer delightfully declared that interest in meditation was currently *exploding*. This explosion in Western culture is very real and unprecedented.

In the West, mysticism has always been restricted to a tiny fraction of the population (i.e., shamans, esoteric brotherhoods, etc.). Never before has there been a widespread teaching of these methods to everyone but rather just to a small spiritual elite group. Now, mysticism pervades the Western world.

The first such book to reach a broad audience was *Creative Visualization* by Shakti Gawain. One could rightfully call this book a practical mystics bible. Many New Agers can trace their first involvement in metaphysics back to this book. Since its publication in 1978, it has sold six million copies and has influenced the fields of psychology, health, business and athletics.[22]

The book became so popular because it addressed such topics as creativity, career goals, relationships, better health, and simply being more relaxed and peaceful. Who wouldn't want to have all this, especially if all it takes is engaging in a simple practice.

Gawain spelled out very clearly what that practice entailed. She taught her readers:

> Almost any form of meditation will eventually take you to an experience of yourself as source, or your higher self …Eventually you will start experiencing certain moments during your meditation when there is a sort of "click" in your consciousness and you feel like things are really working;

you may even experience a lot of energy flowing
through you or a warm radiant glow in your body.
These are signs that you are beginning to channel
the energy of your higher self.[23]

There had been books like hers before, but those appealed to
people already in the New Age subculture. This wasn't true of
Creative Visualization. This book had just the right secular slant on
something inherently spiritual. One could stay a Jew, Catholic or
Protestant and still practice the teachings of the book. All you
were doing was developing yourself not changing your religion.

Shakti Gawain was merely the forerunner of what has become
a flood of such books. A more recent book, *The Artist's Way* by
Julia Cammeron, which is about the "spiritual path to higher creativity," has sold nearly two million copies in ten years.[24]

As another example of this approach, consider a business in a major West Coast city that sold books, tapes, and videos on *stress reduction*.
The owners were very active in their community. Doctors, therapists
and teachers came to them for help. They gave talks to school faculties,
major corporations and all the major hospitals in their city. Their clientele
tended to be affluent, well-educated professionals and business people
who were interested in personal growth.

Along with stress reduction and self-improvement, another
element was subtly present—*spiritual awareness*. One of the owners wrote how she attended a powerful workshop with "Lazaris"
and discovered that his techniques were "practical and useful."[25]
That did not sound too extraordinary until one finds out that
Lazaris is not a person but a *spirit guide!*

Because of the stereotypes about people who gravitate toward
mystical experiences (such as counterculture types), we may tend
to assume people associated with these practices have strange per-
sonalities or are in other ways offbeat. On the contrary, these
individuals are bright, articulate, well dressed, and above all, extremely personable. They are positive, and people gravitate toward
them. A newspaper reporter who did an article on one of them

told me, "She was one of the most calm, serene persons I have ever met." The reporter added, "People want what she has."

It is increasingly evident that many people want this also. The health, self-help, and recovery sections of secular bookstores are now saturated with New Age metaphysical books. Christian columnist Terry Mattingly summed up the situation brilliantly when he observed: "The New Age didn't crest, it soaked in … It is now the dominant theme in commercial bookstores."[26] If the self-help and personal growth sections of most secular commercial bookstores were examined, the only conclusion to come away with would be that New Age mysticism is the prominent spiritual viewpoint of this country.

A case in point: One day while strolling through a shopping mall, I noticed a New Age bookstore and a secular chain bookstore just around the corner from each other. Upon examination, it was clear the secular bookstore had far more New Age books than the New Age bookstore did—hundreds more. Moreover, the vast majority was not in the New Age section but in the self-help and health sections. In essence, New Age bookstores have been rendered redundant by the explosion of practical mystic books stocked in secular ones.

I believe this trend will increase dramatically because of the many centers (one could call practical mystic seminaries) around the country which offer training in meditation to a wide variety of professionals, mostly in the helping professions. Several have quite a large alumni. The Omega Center in Rhinebeck, New York trains 25,000 persons per year.[27] The Kripalu Center in Massachusetts teaches around 14,000 people per year,[28] and at the Interface Center in the Boston area, 20,000 were taught yearly.[29] The tens of thousands emerging from these transformation centers are going to reach and interact with literally millions of people seeking help for the panoply of life's problems.

If you still think the New Age movement is a collection of strange cults populated by aging hippies, emotional cripples, and assorted odd balls who are being duped by money-hungry charlatans and egocentric frauds, then think again. We are not dealing with fringe religious groups or New Age riffraff anymore but with a broad-based effort to influence and restructure our whole society.

Behind this restructuring is a concept both subtle and brilliant. Rather than create competing institutions, as is the case with cults, the goal is to transform existing institutions. One writer explained it as, "…a new society forming within the heart of the old."[30] This has frequently been referred to as a *paradigm shift*. Paradigm means model, as in outlook or viewpoint. The goal of this worldview is to move more and more people to believe they can achieve contact and guidance from the higher self. This will eventually translate into a broad-based cultural shift in which the mystical state will become as common as watching television or reading a newspaper. It will be the predominant model or paradigm for humanity. We are in the midst of this change now. It is not just a fad!

Modern Day Wizards

From a Christian perspective, it becomes obvious this paradigm shift to the public's greater acceptance of New Age teachings is a very dangerous opponent to Christianity's core message. One New Age proponent made this clear when he noted that meditation "brings with it a curious kind of knowing that there is somebody else there with you; you are not alone."[31] One woman who came under this influence shared the instructions she received during meditation. Her guide told her: "I love you, … Stay in my light, my love … Trust in me, your Lord. "[32]

This, I believe, is a classic example of what Leviticus 19:31 warned: "Regard not them that have familiar spirits, neither seek after wizards, to be defiled by them: I am the Lord your God" (KJV).

It is important to note that the word *wizard* in Hebrew means a knowing one. New Age mystic Jacquelyn Small proclaimed: "People who seek spirituality through an inner pathway [meditation] become knowers."[33] In essence, New Agers are wizards!

New Age mysticism reflects the teachings of what were once called the *mystery schools* of antiquity. The mystery religions were so labeled because their teachings were kept hidden from the common people. In fact, the term *occult* originated from the mystery religions because the majority of the people were ignorant of their true meanings. The word occult literally means hidden. The priests and adepts (initiated through various grades or levels) were the ones who gained insight into these hidden truths of the universe. Despite enormous geographical distances and cultural differences, the mysteries all taught the same message: "Happy and blessed one, you have become divine instead of mortal."[34]

When a Christian hears someone claim to be God he immediately recognizes the pronouncements of Satan: "You will be like God" (Gen. 3:5), and "I will be like the Most High" (Isaiah 14:14). The sad thing about this is these experiences are so real and convincing. People experiencing the *superconscious* testify that deep meditative states are very beautiful. They experience intense light flooding them, as did Goodhart, and have a sense of infinite wisdom. In this state, they experience ecstasy and feel a sense of *unity with everything.*

New Age leader Peter Caddy related an incident in which a group of Christians confronted him and tried, as he put it, to "save my soul." He told them to come back and talk to him when they had the same wonderful mystical experiences he had. His point was that these naive Christians had no idea what the metaphysical life was all about and if they did, they would want it.

Feelings such as these are common in New Age circles and have hooked many into thinking something this positive *has* to be of God. The truth of the matter is, those who say they have connected with their divinity and are God, sadly, have joined the ranks of those who: "Professing to be wise [knowing the truth], they became fools [absurd], and changed the glory of the incorruptible God into an image made like corruptible man ..." (Romans 1:22-23).

One New Age spiritual writer told her readers: When Christians ask if "you believe you are a sinner," respond with, "We have not perfectly realized our divine potential, but are still in the process of unfolding it through meditation and higher states of consciousness."[35]

One person who claimed to have reached his higher self was

Swami Muktnanda, one of the most admired and respected New Age leaders during the 1970s and early 1980s. Many thought he was the virtual embodiment of the *God-realized* master. He told his disciples: "Kneel to your own self. Honor and worship your own Being. Chant the mantra always going on within you. Meditate on your own self. God dwells within you as you."[36]

But when Muktananda died in 1983, one of his closest followers revealed that his master "ended as a feebleminded, sadistic tyrant luring devout little girls to his bed every night with promises of grace and self-realization."[37] Without realizing he was echoing the truth of the Bible, the disciple concluded:

> There is no absolute assurance that enlightenment necessitates the moral virtue of a person. There is no guarantee against the weakness of anger, lust and greed in the human soul. The enlightened are on an equal footing with the ignorant in the struggle against their own evil.[38]

Swami Muktananda's "enlightenment" did not translate into personal righteousness. He was just a sinner who mystically perceived he was God.

The Cross vs. The Higher Self

The New Age and Christianity definitely clash on the answer to this question of human imperfection. New Age metaphysics espouses the doctrine of becoming self-realized, united with the universe, which New Agers see as God, but in reality it is the realm of familiar spirits, led by Lucifer himself. On the other hand, the gospel Christians embrace offers salvation to humanity through grace (unmerited favor). Romans 3:24 boldly states: " ... being justified freely by His grace through the redemption that is in Christ Jesus." In Romans 6:23 we read: "For the wages of sin is death, but the gift of God is eternal life in Christ Jesus our Lord."

This gift is not earned or given as a reward for earnest or good intention. Ephesians 2:8-9 states clearly: "For by grace you have been saved through faith, and that not of yourselves; it is the gift of God; not of works, lest anyone should boast."

This Scripture suggests that the issue of pride divides all of man's religions from Christianity. Religion persuades us that man is innately good and, therefore, can earn his way to heaven through human perfectibility or, better yet, through the realization of his own divinity. Christianity emphatically states the opposite view that man needs to humbly recognize his own sinfulness and fallibility, and consequently the need of salvation through grace.

Scripture then takes those who recognize their own sinfulness and presents to them God's solution—salvation through the Cross: "In Him we have redemption through His blood, the forgiveness of sins, according to the riches of His grace" (Ephesians 1:7). In Romans 10: 9, 10 Paul extends God's invitation, " ... if you confess with your mouth the Lord Jesus and believe in your heart that God has raised Him from the dead, you will be saved." Salvation is entirely a gift of grace bestowed on whoever will believe in Jesus' sacrifice on the Cross as the God-man. Consequently we must receive Him as Lord and Savior with the understanding that it is by grace and grace alone that we are made acceptable in Christ before a holy God. Justification is God's gift to the believer. This saving faith, a demonstration of His faithfulness, is more than an intellectual belief in Jesus' death on the Cross but involves committing and entrusting one's life to Jesus as both Lord and Savior understanding that Christ's going to the Cross was a finished work and we as believers are now complete in Him. Nothing else can be added to this. How totally opposite from New Age thinking is God's plan of salvation!

It all comes down to the preaching of the higher self versus *the preaching of the Cross.* New Agers say God is synonymous with a person's higher self, and the experience of God is discovered through the way of meditation. The Christian proclaims his sinfulness before a Holy God and remembers he is but dust, saved only by the grace of God through the sacrificial shedding of Christ's blood for his sins.

The message of Jesus Christ reaches past the degenerate state of humanity with the love of God who sacrificed His only begotten Son for the Swami Muktanandas of the world. The Bible teaches that man has a basic rebellious and ungodly nature (which is evident), and his ways are naturally self-centered and evil in the sight of God, but Scripture does not teach that God ignores us. Christ dying for the ungodly to reconcile the repenting sinner to God reveals the Lord's love toward man.

This explains why Christianity must be steadfast on these issues. If a belief system does not teach the preaching of the Cross, then it is not "the power of God" (I Cor. 1:18). If other ways are correct, then Christ died in vain, His blood unnecessary.

Because of this conflict, one would certainly think Christendom would be the most formidable obstacle to the New Age, standing like a bulwark against this tide of meditation teachers and practical mystics. But, incredibly, it is becoming increasingly apparent that the most successful practical mystics are appearing from within Christendom itself. Instead of retarding the momentum of New Age spirituality, it is our own churches that may very well be the decisive catalysts, which propel the New Age into prominence. Certain spiritual practices are becoming entrenched in our churches that, like an iceberg, seem beautiful and impressive on the surface but can nevertheless cause great damage to the impact of the gospel of Jesus Christ.

2

The Yoga of the West

One day, I wandered into a secular bookstore to investigate their religion section. The section was divided into two equal parts. The one on the left had the heading *Spirituality: New Age*. It accordingly contained titles reflecting that viewpoint. On the right was *Spirituality: Judeo-Christian*. In this section, one would expect to find titles in line with traditional concepts of Judeo-Christian orthodoxy. Not so! The basic principles of the New Age movement were represented, with only a few exceptions, in both parts. How is this possible?

Roman Catholic writer William Johnston answered how when he penned the following observation:

> [S]omething very powerful is emerging ... we are witnessing a spiritual revolution of great magnitude in the whole world ... the rise of a new school of mysticism within Christianity ... It is growing year by year.[1]

That bookstore represented a perfect example of this new school of mysticism. Where there had always been a clear difference between Eastern spirituality and Christianity, that line had now become blurred.

For the most part, the evangelical church has very little awareness of this rapidly growing spiritual revolution. Most evangelicals seem unaware there has even been a paradigm shift in spirituality.

This is understandable since most people do not know much of what goes on beyond their own circles. Historically, God's people have been slow in responding to the shifts that occur in culture. A consequence of this naiveté is a growing spillover effect from this phenomenon into the evangelical church, appealing to those who hunger for ways to walk closer with God. Many Christians sincerely desire to have more full and satisfying spiritual lives for themselves and their loved ones. Thus, it is imperative Christians come to a clear understanding of just what *is* the nature of this mystical thinking and why it resonates with New Age thought.

Christian Samadhi

None other than Alice Bailey, the famous occult prophetess who coined the term New Age, made this startling pronouncement: "It is, of course, easy to find many passages which link the way of the Christian Knower with that of his brother in the East. They bear witness to the same efficacy of method."[2]

What did she mean by the term "Christian Knower"? The answer is unmistakable! In the first chapter we saw occultism is awakening the *mystical faculties* to see God as the a*ll in all.* In Hinduism this is called reaching *samadhi* or enlightenment. It is the final objective of yoga meditation: God in everything—a force or power flowing through *all* that exists.

William Johnston believes such an experience exists within the context of Christianity. He explains:

> What I can safely say, however, is that there is a Christian samadhi that has always occupied an honored place in the spirituality of the West. This, I believe, is the thing that is nearest to Zen. It is this that I have called Christian Zen.[3]

The famous psychologist Carl Jung predicted this system would be the *yoga of the west.* [4]

Christian zen? Christian yoga? These seem like oxymorons—like military pacifism or alcoholic sobriety. Christians, conservative ones at least, have always viewed these concepts as heretical and anti-Christian. The word most commonly used for it is *pantheism—all is God*. But when one looks at the *Christian* zen movement one discovers a similar term, which for all practical purposes, means the same thing. This term is called *panentheism—God is in all things*.

A highly respected source, *The Evangelical Dictionary of Theology*, defines panentheism as a worldview that combines "the strengths of classic theism with the strengths of classic pantheism."[5] With panentheism you still have a personal God (theism) coupled with God's pervasive presence in all creation (pantheism). In other words, with panentheism God is both a personality and an all encompassing substance as opposed to God being an impersonal substance that incorporates all of creation as found in pantheism.

The credibility of *A Time of Departing* rests on whether or not panentheism has a legitimate place in orthodox Christianity. This is a vital question because panentheism is the foundational worldview among those who engage in mystical prayer. Fr. Ken Kaisch, a teacher of mystical prayer, made this very clear in his book, *Finding God*, where he noted: "The first and most important result [of this prayer] is an increasing sense of God's Presence *in all things*" (emphasis mine).[6]

Here lies the core of panentheism: God is in everything and everything is in God. The only difference between pantheism and panentheism is *how* God is in everything.

This position of the panentheist is challenging to understand. Your outer personality is not God, but God is still in you as your true identity. This explains why mystics say, *all is one*. At the mystical level they experience this God-force that seems to flow through everything and everybody. All has God in it, as a living, vital presence. It is just hidden.

The theological implications of this worldview put it at direct odds with Biblical Christianity for obvious reasons. Only one true God exists, and His identity is not in everyone. The fullness of

God's identity, in bodily form, rests in Jesus Christ and Him only!

> For in Him [Christ] dwells all the fullness of the God-
> head bodily; and you are complete in Him, who is the
> head of all principality and power. (Colossians 2:9-10)

Scripture clearly teaches the only deity in man is Christ who dwells in the heart of the born again believer. Further, Jesus made it clear not everyone will be born again—having God's Spirit (John 3). Yet the panentheist perceives every person and everything has the identity of God within them.

William Johnston again states: "For God is the core of my being and the core of all beings."[7] This fundamentally alleviates believing the gospel as the avenue to reconciliation with God, because God is already there. It effectively leaves out the finished work of Christ as the binding agent and is contrary to the following verses:

> For the message of the cross is foolishness to those
> who are perishing, but to us who are being saved it
> is the power of God. (I Cor. 1:18)

> Whoever transgresses and does not abide in the doc-
> trine of Christ does not have God. He who abides
> in the doctrine of Christ has both the Father and
> the Son. (II John 9)

The Bible does reveal though that God upholds all things with His omnipresence but He does not do this by being *the substance of* all things. The word of God also says, "for in Him [Christ] we live and move and have our being ..." (Acts 17:28). But this means *of Him*. The belief that God indwells everything is simply heresy. God will not, and cannot share His personal essence with anyone or anything outside of the Trinity. Even Christians are only partakers of the Divine Nature and not *possessors* of the Divine Nature. 2 Peter 1:3-4 says:

[A]s His divine power has given to us all things that
pertain to life and godliness, through the knowledge
of Him who called us by glory and virtue, by which
have been given to us exceedingly great and precious
promises, that through these you may be *partakers* of
the divine nature, having escaped the corruption that
is in the world through lust (emphasis mine).

Here the apostle Peter is writing to Christians, not the world.
He acknowledges the *participation* of the believer with the work
of the Holy Spirit. The word partaker is taken from the Greek
word koinonos, which means a sharer (associate), companion or
fellowship partner. In other words, the born again believer shares
in the promises of the purifying work of the Holy Spirit and the
definite break with the corruption caused by an evil world. Moreover, a partaker or participant is one who has been invited and
makes a decision to become involved (i.e., born again through
faith). A possessor, on the other hand, is one who is already in
possession of something. In the case of the panentheist and pan-
theist, the possession they are claiming *is God*. They do not believe a fundamental change is needed, just an awareness of what
is already there.

This conclusion becomes quite obvious when we examine such
passages as Isaiah 42:8: "I am the Lord, that is my name; and My
glory I will not give to another, …" Creation can *reflect* God's glory
(Isaiah 6:3), but it can never *possess* God's glory. For to do that
would mean God indeed giving His glory to another.

Those who support this heresy draw the same conclusion of mystical
panentheism that has been articulated by author Willigis Jager: "The physical
world, human beings, and everything that is are all forms of the Ultimate
Reality, all expressions of God, all 'one with the Father.'"[8] He means not all
Christians but *all people*. This is nothing less than Hindu samadhi with Christian
spray paint. Those in this movement who are honest have no qualms about
acknowledging this—as one did so aptly when he confessed: "The meditation
of advanced occultists is identical with the prayer of advanced mystics."[9]

The Language of God is Silence

For many years during my research I would come across the term *contemplative prayer*. Immediately I disregarded it as having any New Age connotation because I thought it meant to ponder while praying—which is the normal association with that term. But in the New Age field, things may not always be what they seem to untrained ears.

What contemplative prayer actually entails is described very clearly by the following writer:

> When one enters the deeper layers of contemplative prayer one sooner or later experiences the void, the emptiness, the nothingness ... the profound mystical silence ... an absence of thought.[10]

To my dismay I discovered this *mystical silence* is accomplished by the same methods used by New Agers to achieve their silence—the mantra and the breath! Contemplative prayer is the repetition of what is referred to as a *prayer word* or *sacred word* until one reaches a state where the soul, rather than the mind, contemplates God. Contemplative prayer teacher Willigis Jager brought this out when he instructed:

> Do not reflect on the meaning of the word; thinking and reflecting must cease, as all mystical writers insist. Simply "sound" the word silently, letting go of all feelings and thoughts.[11]

Those with some theological training may recognize this teaching as the historical stream going back centuries to such figures as Meister Eckart, Teresa of Avila, John of the Cross, and Julian of Norwich.

One of the most well known writings on the subject is the classic 14th century treatise, *The Cloud of Unknowing*, written by an anonymous author. It is essentially a manual on contemplative prayer issuing such instructions as: "Take just a little word, of one syllable rather than of two … With this word you are to strike down every kind of thought under the cloud of forgetting."[12]

The premise here is that God can never be really known in a conventional non-mystical way. Therefore, the mind has to be *shut-down, turned-off* so one can enter the cloud of unknowing where the presence of God awaits. The practitioners of this method believe if the sacred words are Christian, you will get Christ—it is simply a matter of intent.

Contemplative prayer may sound exotic and appealing, but it is Biblically groundless.

Many instances throughout the Bible describe godly men and women having had mystical experiences with the Lord or His messengers. However, I see no evidence anywhere of mystics found in the godly camp. Let me explain.

Legitimate mysticism was always initiated *by* God to certain individuals for certain revelations and was never based on a method for the changing of consciousness. In Acts, Peter fell into a trance while in prayer (Acts 11:5). But it was God, not Peter, who initiated the trance and facilitated it.

A mystic, on the other hand, is someone who uses rote methods in an attempt to meet God. Those who use this method put themselves in a trance without God's sanction. This approach is extremely dangerous. Nowhere in the Bible is such a mystical practice prescribed. Without a doubt, the Lord for the purpose of teaching people a respect for God's holiness and His plans ordered certain ceremonies for His people (especially in the Old Testament). Nonetheless, Scripture contains no reference in which God ordered mystical practices. The gifts of the Spirit spoken of in the New Testament were supernatural in nature but did not fall under the parameters of mysticism. God bestowed spiritual gifts without the Christian practicing a method beforehand to get God's response.

Proponents of contemplative prayer would respond with: What about the verses in Psalms that speak of *being still* and knowing God? On the surface, this argument can seem very valid. But once the meaning of still is examined, any contemplative connection is expelled. The word means to slacken, to cease or abate. In other words, the context is to slow down and trust God rather than get in a dither over things. Relax and watch God work.

It should also be pointed out that being born again, in and of itself, is a mystical experience. But this experience is a direct act by God upon those who have put their faith in Jesus Christ. The Holy Spirit has regenerated the once-dead spirit of man to a living spirit with God. Christianity is not a philosophy or even a religion but a direct experience with God. One is "passed from death into life" (John 5:24).

Nowhere in the Bible is the silence referred to as the "power of God," but faith in the "message of the cross" (1 Cor. 1:18) most certainly is!

Extent

As I stated in the beginning of the chapter, many evangelical Christians are not even aware that a practical Christian mystical movement exists, let alone know the scope of it. If they have heard of it, it is usually only in a vague sense.

I once attempted to inform a Baptist pastor about these issues. He responded with a thinly veiled skepticism and politely patronized me. His reasoning was this: If what I was telling him was true, it certainly would be widely known in evangelical circles. Since it was not, I must be exaggerating the scale and influence of this movement for sensationalistic effect.

Yet, evidence of the magnitude of this mystical prayer is within reach of the average person. In fact, Newsweek magazine did a cover story called "Talking to God," which made a clear reference to it. The article disclosed:

> [S]ilence, appropriate body posture and, above all, *emptying the mind* through *repetition* of prayer—have been the practices of mystics in all the great world

religions. And they form the basis on which most
modern *spiritual directors* guide those who want to
draw closer to God. (emphasis mine)[13]

It is amazing to me how Newsweek clearly observed this
shift in the spiritual paradigm while many Christians (even some
of our leaders) still live in ignorance of this change. Are the
teachings of the practical Christian mystic actually being assimilated so well even our pastors are not discerning this shift?

The most obvious integration of this movement can be found
predominantly, though not exclusively, in the following two traditions. The first and foremost is Roman Catholicism. Michael Leach,
former president of the *Catholic Book Publishers Association*, made
this incredibly candid assertion:

But many people also believe that the spiritual principles underlying the New Age movement will soon
be incorporated—or rather reincorporated—into the
mainstream of Catholic belief. In fact, it's happening in the United States right now.[14]

Incorporating it is! And it is assimilating primarily through the
contemplative prayer movement.

Contemplative leader Basil Pennington acknowledging its size
said: "We are part of an immensely large community … 'We are
Legion.'"[15] Backing him up, a major Catholic resource company
stated: "Contemplative prayer has once again become commonplace in the Christian community …"[16]

Another highly respected and well-known Catholic priest, William Shannon, went so far as to say contemplative spirituality has
now widely replaced old-style Catholicism.[17] This is not to say the
Mass or any of the sacraments have been abandoned, but the underlying spiritual worldview of many in the Catholic church is now
contemplative in its orientation.

One of my personal experiences with the saturation of mysticism in the Catholic church was in a phone conversation I had with the head nun at a local retreat center. She told me the same message Shannon conveys. The nun made it clear *The Cloud of Unknowing* is now the basis for nearly all Catholic spirituality, and contemplative prayer is now becoming widespread all over the world.

I had always been confused as to the real nature of this advance in the Catholic church. Was this just the work of a few mavericks and renegades, or did the church hierarchy sanction this practice? My concerns were affirmed when I read in an interview that the mystical prayer movement not only had the approval of the highest echelons of Catholicism but also was, in fact, the *source* of its expansion. Speaking of a meeting between Pope Paul and members of the Catholic Trappist Monastic Order in the 1970s, a leading contemplative teacher, Thomas Keating, disclosed the following:

> The Pontiff declared that unless the Church rediscovered the contemplative tradition, renewal couldn't take place. He specifically called upon the monastics, because they lived the contemplative life, to help the laity and those in other religious orders bring that dimension into their lives as well.[18]

Just look at the latest official catechism of the Catholic church to see contemplative prayer officially endorsed and promoted to the faithful by the powers that be. The new catechism firmly states: "Contemplative prayer is hearing the word of God ... Contemplative prayer is Silence."[19]

I realized just how successfully Pope Paul's admonitions have been carried out when I discovered the following at one popular Catholic bookstore. Many shelves were marked as *spirituality*—the focal point of the entire store. Eighty to ninety percent of the books on those shelves were on mystical prayer. It was clearly the overriding theme.

In response to this turnabout, non-mystic Catholics have become very alarmed at what is happening to their church. What seems to be a glorious renewal to those like Shannon is viewed by other Catholics as a slide into apostasy.

One Catholic layman who is outspoken about this is author Randy England. In his book, *Unicorn In the Sanctuary*, England made plain just how pervasive these practices are in his church. He warned:

> The struggle is difficult. It is more likely than not that your pastor is open to New Age ideas …Even Catholics with no interest in New Age practices are becoming accustomed to its concepts; they should be well primed by the time Creation-Centered Spirituality becomes the norm in our churches.[20]

It is apparent that a pope was responsible for what Randy England and others like him are witnessing in their church. This is not an aberration—a wandering from the church but part of the program from the top down.

The second Christian tradition moving towards the contemplative camp is the so-called mainline Protestant tradition (Episcopalians, United Methodists, Presbyterians, Lutherans, United Church of Christ, etc.). Not all mainline churches have embraced the contemplative movement, but their deep tradition of twentieth century liberalism and social-political activism have left them spiritually dry and thirsting for supernatural experiences. This school of practical mysticism gives them a sense of spirituality while still allowing them a liberal, political correctness.

A sales person at a bookstore that caters to these denominations once told me the contemplative prayer view has found a large audience in the Protestant mainstream, and many pastors are very open to these practices. She added that some members of the clergy did show resistance, but a clear momentum towards the contemplative direction was occurring. An article in *Publisher's Weekly* magazine addressing the move toward contemplative prayer in mainstream religious circles backed up her observation. One woman in the publishing field was quoted as saying, "[M]any Protestants are looking to satisfy that yearning by a return to the Western contemplative tradition."[21] Another college professor pointed out:

> My students have been typically middle-aged and upper middle class Methodists, Presbyterians, Congregationalists, and Baptists, active in the lay leadership of their churches. To outward appearances, they are quite conventional people. Yet I have found that virtually every one of my students has encountered the new age in one of its many forms and has been attracted by its mystery.[22]

Contemplative spirituality provides a seemingly profound experience of God without having to adhere to a conservative social outlook. It also gives the practitioners comfort to know they draw on a so-called Christian well of tradition. This dilutes any reluctance some might have about the orthodoxy of these practices.

A Borrowing From the East

Catholic priest William Shannon in his book, *Seeds of Peace*, explained the human dilemma as being the following:

> This forgetfulness, of our oneness with God, is not just a personal experience, it is the corporate experience of humanity. Indeed, this is one way to understanding original sin. *We are in God, but we don't seem to know it. We are in paradise, but we don't realize it.*[23]

Shannon's viewpoint defines the basic underlying worldview of the contemplative prayer movement as a whole. One can find similar quotations in practically every book written by contemplative authors. A Hindu guru or a zen Buddhist master would offer the same explanation. This conclusion becomes completely logical when tracing the *roots* of contemplative prayer. Let us look at the beginnings of this practice.

In the early Middle Ages, there lived a group of hermits in the wilderness areas of the Middle East. They were known to history as the *desert fathers*. They dwelt in small isolated communities for the purpose of devoting their lives completely to God without distraction. The contemplative movement traces its roots back to these monks. They were the ones who first promoted the mantra as a *prayer tool*. One meditation scholar made this connection when he said:

> The meditation practices and rules for living of these earliest Christian monks bear strong similarity to those of their Hindu and Buddhist renunciate brethren several kingdoms to the East ... the meditative techniques they adopted for finding their God suggest either a borrowing from the East or a spontaneous rediscovery.[24]

Many of the desert fathers, in their zeal, were simply seeking God through trial and error. A leading contemplative prayer teacher candidly acknowledged the haphazard way the desert fathers acquired their practices:

> It was a time of great experimentation with spiritual methods. Many different kinds of disciplines were tried, some of which are too harsh or extreme for people today. Many different methods of prayer were created and explored by them.[25]

Certain spiritual endeavors can be experimented with and come out refined, while other ventures can have disastrous results. Attempting to reach God through occult mystical practices is one experiment that will guarantee disaster. The desert fathers of Egypt were located in a particularly dangerous locale at that time to be groping around for innovative approaches to God, because as one theologian pointed out:

> [D]evelopment of Christian meditative disciplines
> should have begun in Egypt because much of the
> intellectual, philosophical, and theological basis of
> the practice of meditation in Christianity also comes
> out of the theology of Hellenic and Roman Egypt.
> This is significant because it was in Alexandria that
> Christian theology had the most contact with the
> various Gnostic speculations which, according to
> many scholars, have their roots in the East, possi-
> bly in India.[26]

Consequently, the desert fathers believed as long as the desire for God was sincere—anything could be utilized to reach God. If a method worked for the Hindus to reach their gods, then Christian mantras could be used to reach Jesus. A current practitioner and promoter of the desert fathers' mystical prayer still echoes the logical formulations of his mystical ancestors:

> In the wider ecumenism of the Spirit being opened
> for us today, we need to humbly accept the learnings
> of particular Eastern religions … What makes a par-
> ticular practice Christian is not its source, but its intent
> … this is important to remember in the face of those
> Christians who would try to impoverish our spiritual
> resources by too narrowly defining them. If we view
> the human family as one in God's spirit, then this his-
> torical cross-fertilization is not surprising … selective
> attention to Eastern spiritual practices can be of great
> assistance to a fully embodied Christian life.[27]

Do you catch the reasoning here? Non-Christian sources, as avenues to spiritual growth, are perfectly legitimate in the Christian life, and if Christians only practice their Christianity based on the Bible, they will impoverish their spirituality. This was the thinking of the desert fathers. So as a result we now have contemplative prayer.

Please take to heart what Jesus Christ expressly warned His disciples in Matthew 6:7: "And when you pray, do not use vain repetitions, as the heathen do."

It should be apparent that mantra meditation or *sacred word* prayer qualifies as "vain repetition" and clearly fits an accurate description of the point Jesus was making here. Yet in spite of this, responsible evangelical Christians have often pronounced that Christian mysticism is different from other forms of mysticism (such as Eastern or occult) because it is focused on Jesus Christ.

This logic may sound credible on the surface, but Christians must ask a simple question: What really makes a practice Christian? The answer is obvious: Did Christ sanction it? A Christian is one who is a disciple (pupil) of Jesus Christ. This means, as a Christian, I am to follow the teachings of Jesus Christ. Would Jesus hold out on me? Never! Jesus wants us to live a life resulting in communicating the good news of salvation to a dying world.

Understanding this truth, God has declared in His Word what He wants from us. He does not leave it up to earnest yet sinful people to invent their own Christianity. When Christians ignore God's instructions in following Him they end up learning *the way of the heathen*. Israel did this countless times. It is just human nature.

A classic Biblical example of spiritual infidelity can be seen in the account of Cain and Abel. Both of Adam's sons wanted to please God, but Cain decided he would experiment with his own method of being devout. Cain must have reasoned to himself: "Perhaps God would like the fruit better than a dead animal. It's not as gross. It's less smelly. Hey, I think I will try it!"

As you know, God was not the least bit entertained by Cain's attempt to create his own approach to God's acceptance. The Lord made it clear to Cain that God's favor would be upon him if he *did what is right*, not just what focused on God.

In many ways the desert fathers were like Cain—eager to please but not willing to listen to the instruction of the Lord and do what is right. One cannot fault them for their devotion, but one certainly can for their lack of discernment.

New Age or Christian?

Before writing this book I made sure I could prove, beyond a doubt, that contemplative prayer was not only *not* part of the faith, which is easily done but to also prove it *is* an integral part of the New Age movement. In fact, New Agers see contemplative prayer as one of their own practices. Why would both New Agers and Christians claim contemplative prayer as their own? Certainly, you will not find the New Age movement promoting someone like Francis Schaeffer or Charles Spurgeon, but you will find many instances such as the following:

> New Age therapist Jacquelyn Small lists contemplative prayer as a gateway to the spirituality to which she belongs. She explains it as: "A form of Christian meditation, its practitioners are trained to focus on an inner symbol that quiets the mind … When practitioners become skilled at this method of meditation, they undergo a deep trance state similar to auto-hypnosis."[28]

The editors of the magazine *New Age Journal* have put together a book entitled: *As Above, So Below*—which they promote as a handbook on "Paths to Spiritual Renewal," according to their worldview. Along with chapters on shamanism, goddess worship and wholistic health, there is a chapter devoted to contemplative prayer. In it they proudly declare: "Those who have practiced Transcendental Meditation may be surprised to learn that Christianity has its own time-honored form of mantra meditation … Reliance on a mantric centering device had a long history in the mystical canon of Christianity."[29]

New Age author Tav Sparks lays out an array of *doorways* in one chapter of his book, *The Wide Open Door*. Again, along with a variety of occult and Eastern practices we find what Sparks calls *Spiritual Christianity*. He says: "The good news is that there are some forms of Christianity today that are alive with spiritual power." He then uses a few contemplative prayer advocates as examples.[30]

Perhaps the most compelling example of all is one by a foremost figure in the contemplative prayer movement itself, Tilden

Edwards. Edwards leads the prestigious Shalem Prayer Institute in Washington D.C.—a center which turns out spiritual directors from its training programs. In his book, *Spiritual Friend*, he suggests those who practice contemplative prayer and have begun experiencing "spiritual unfolding" and other "unusual experiences," should turn to a book entitled, *Psychosynthesis*, in order to understand the "dynamics" at "certain stages."[31] For the Christian there is a major problem with this advice. The book Edwards recommends is a book written by a world famous occultist, Roberto Assagioli.

These dynamics for certain stages of "spiritual unfolding" may be great for those in tune with occultism, but remember, Edwards is guiding Christians toward this form of prayer. Edwards himself puts to rest any pretense that this is *truly* Christian when he openly admits: "This mystical stream [contemplative prayer] is the Western bridge to Far Eastern spirituality."[32]

In answer to the well-meaning but folly-laden attempts of the desert fathers and their spiritual descendants, I must refer them to the deep observations of Charles Spurgeon who penned:

> Human wisdom delights to trim and arrange the doctrine of the cross into a system more artificial and more congenial with the depraved tastes of fallen nature; instead, however, of improving the gospel carnal wisdom pollutes it, until it becomes another gospel, and not the truth of God at all. All alterations and amendments of the Lord's own Word are defilements and pollutions.[33]

Christian Kundalini

Many Christians might have great difficulty accepting the assessment that what is termed Christian mysticism is, in truth, not really Christian. They might feel this rejection is spawned by a heresy hunting mentality completely ignoring the love and devotion of God that also accompanies the mystical life. To those who are still skeptical, I suggest examining the writings of Philip St. Romain, who wrote a book about his journey into contemplative prayer called *Kundalini Energy and Christian Spirituality*. This title is insightful because kundalini is a Hindu term for the mystical power or force that underlies their spirituality. In Hinduism it is commonly referred to as *the serpent power*.

Philip St. Romain, a substance abuse counselor and devout Catholic lay minister, began his journey while practicing contemplative prayer or *resting in the still point*, as he called it. What happened to him following this practice should bear the utmost scrutiny from the evangelical community—especially from our leadership. The future course of evangelical Christianity rests on whether St. Romain's path is just a fluke or if it is the norm for contemplative spirituality.

Having rejected mental prayer as "unproductive,"[34] he embraced the prayer form that switches off the mind, creating what he described as a mental passivity. What he encountered next underscores my concern with sobering clarity:

> Then came the lights! The gold swirls that I had noted on occasion began to intensify, forming themselves into patterns that both intrigued and captivated me … There were always four or five of these; as soon as one would fade, another would appear, even brighter and more intense … They came through complete passivity and only after I had been *in the silence* for a while (emphasis mine).[35]

After this, St. Romain began to sense "wise sayings" coming into his mind and felt he was "receiving messages from another."[36] He also had physical developments occur during his periods in the silence. He would feel "prickly sensations" on the top of his head and at times it would "fizzle with energy."[37] This sensation would go on for days. The culmination of St. Romain's mystical excursion was predictable: When you do *Christian yoga* or *Christian zen* you end up with *Christian samadhi* as did he. He proclaimed: "No longer is there any sense of alienation, for the Ground that flows throughout my being is identical with the Reality of all creation. It seems that the mystics of all the world's religions know something of this."[38] St. Romain, logically, passed on to the next stage with:

> [T]he significance of this work, perhaps, lies in its potential to contribute to the dialogue between Christianity and Eastern forms of mysticism such as are promoted in what is called New Age spirituality.[39]

Many people believe St. Romain is a devout Christian. He claims he loves Jesus, believes in salvation and is a member in good standing within his church. What changed though were his sensibilities. He revealed:

> I cannot make any decisions for myself without the approbation of the inner adviser, whose voice speaks so clearly in times of need ... there is a distinct sense of an inner eye of some kind "seeing" with my two sense eyes ...[40]

St. Romain would probably be astounded that somebody would question his claims to finding truth because of the positive nature of his mysticism. But is this "inner adviser" St. Romain has connected with really God? This is a fair question to ask especially when this prayer method is starting to spread within a broad spectrum of Christianity.

As articulated earlier in this chapter, this practice has already spread extensively throughout the Roman Catholic and Protestant mainline churches. It has now crossed over and is manifesting itself in conservative denominations as well—ones that have traditionally stood against the New Age. Just as secular society has been hit by a tidal wave of practical mystics, so also has the religious world. St. Romain makes one observation in his book that I take very seriously. Like his secular practical mystic brethren, he has a strong sense of mission and destiny. He predicts:

> Could it be that those who make the journey to the True Self are, in some ways, demonstrating what lies in store for the entire race? What a magnificent world that would be—for the majority of people to be living out of the True Self state. Such a world cannot come, however, unless hundreds of thousands of people experience the regression of the Ego in the service of transcendence [meditation], and then restructure the culture to accommodate similar growth for millions of others. I believe we are only now beginning to recognize this task.[41]

A book entitled: *Metaphysical Primer: A Guide to Understanding Metaphysics* outlines the basic laws and principles of the New Age movement. First and foremost is the following principle: "You are one with the Deity, as is all of humanity ... Everything is one with everything else. All that is on Earth is an expression of the One Deity and is permeated with Its energies."[42] St. Romain's statement was: " ... the Ground [God] that flows throughout my being is identical with the Reality of all creation."[43] The two views are *identical!*

St. Romain came to this view through standard contemplative prayer, not zen, not yoga but a *Christian* form of these practices. The lights were also standard procedure as one contemplative author suggested:

> Christian literature makes reference to many episodes that parallel the experiences of those going a yogic way. Saint Anthony, one of the first desert mystics, frequently encountered strange and sometimes terrifying psychophysical forces while at prayer.[44]

Unfortunately, this experience was not confined to St. Anthony alone. This has been the common progression into mystical awareness throughout the centuries, which also means many now entering the contemplative path will follow suit. This is not just empty conjecture. One mystical trainer wrote:

> [T]he classical experience of enlightenment as described by Buddhist monks, Hindu gurus, *Christian mystics*, Aboriginal shamans, Sufi sheiks and Hebrew kabalists is characterized by two universal elements: radiant light and an experience of oneness with creation (emphasis mine).[45]

Without the "radiant light," there can be no oneness. The second always follows the first. Here lies the heart of occultism.

The issue is obviously a serious one to contend with. Many individuals, using terms for themselves like *spiritual director,* are starting to spring up in the evangelical church. Many of them teach the message of mystical prayer.

Pastor and author John MacArthur summed up this profound danger brilliantly in his book, *Reckless Faith:*

> The evangelical consensus has shifted decidedly in the past two decades. Our collective message is now short on doctrine and long on experience. *Thinking* is deemed less important than feeling ... The love of sound doctrine that has always been a distinguishing characteristic of evangelicalism has all but disappeared. Add a dose of mysticism to this mix and you have the recipe for unmitigated spiritual disaster.[46]

Sound doctrine must be central to this debate because New Ageism has a very idealistic side to it, offering a mystical approach to solve human problems. Everyone would like to have their problems solved. Right? That is the practical aspect I wrote about in the last chapter—a seemingly direct route to a happy and fulfilled life. However, one can *promote* the attributes of God without actually *having* God. "Therefore it is no great thing if his [Satan's] ministers also transform themselves into ministers of righteousness, ..." (2 Cor. 11:15). People who promote a presumably godly form of spirituality can indeed come against the truth of Christ. Then how can you be assured what you believe and practice *is* of God?

The Christian message has been clear from the beginning—God has sent a *Savior.* If man only had to practice some kind of mystical prayer to gain access to God then the life, ministry, death, and resurrection of Jesus Christ was a waste of time. Sound Christian doctrine comes from the understanding that mankind is sinful, fallen, and separated from God. Man needs a saving work by God! A teaching like panentheism (God is in everybody) cannot be reconciled to the finished work of Christ. How could Jesus be our Savior then? New Agers will say He is a model for *Christ consciousness*, but the Bible teaches He is the Savior of mankind. Therefore, panentheism cannot be a true doctrine.

The problem is that many well-intentioned people embrace the teachings of panentheism because it sounds so good. It appears less bigoted on God's part. No one is left out—all are connected to God. There is a great appeal in this message. Nevertheless, the Bible does not teach a universal salvation for man. In contrast, Jesus said:

> Enter by the narrow gate; for wide is the gate and broad is the way that leads to destruction, and there are many who go in by it. Because narrow is the gate and difficult is the way which leads to life, and there are few who find it. (Matt. 7:13-14)

Christ's message is the polar opposite of the New Age message and universalist teachings. Many people (even Christians) today think only a few really bad people will be sent to hell. But in Matthew, the words of Jesus make it clear that is just not so.

While God sent His Son, Jesus Christ, to die for the sins of the world, He did not say all would be saved. His words are clear that many would reject the salvation He provided. But for those who are saved, they have been given the "ministry of reconciliation" (2 Cor. 5:18) making an appeal to those who are perishing (2 Cor. 4:3). The Christian message is not samadhi, zen, kundalini, or the contemplative silence. It is the power of the Cross! "For the message of the cross is foolishness to those who are perishing, but to us who are being saved it is the power of God" (1 Cor. 1:18). Yes, perishing, not just unaware of their true self.

In a recent opinion poll, startling evidence describes how Americans actually view God. *Spirituality and Health* magazine hired a reputable pollster organization to gauge the spiritual beliefs of the American public. This national poll revealed that 84 percent of those questioned believed God to be "everywhere and in everything" rather than "someone somewhere."[47] This means panentheism is now the more popular view of God. If true, then a high percentage of evangelical Christians in America already lean towards a panentheistic view of God and without realizing it devalue the very source of their salvation.

3

Proponents and Visionaries

A friend once related to me a conversation he had with a senior pastor of a sizable evangelical church. The pastor shared with him how much he enjoyed the works of one of the figures discussed in this chapter. My friend responded with a substantial concern about the validity of this author's practice of mysticism and shared with him what I had discovered about the contemplative prayer movement. On hearing these concerns the pastor became furious and retorted: "These people [referring to me] just want to tear down everyone; they just want to destroy." He then stormed off in disgust.

This response is quite understandable if you take into account that this pastor obviously perceived something valuable in the writings of this spiritual writer. His respect and admiration for the author automatically rejected anything that resembled criticism. Nevertheless, in spite of this touchiness, the controversy remains valid. Is contemplative spirituality of God or not?

There certainly is a *perceived* presence of God in the contemplative practice as noted by Brother Wayne Teasdale who stated: "[I]n the silence is a dynamic presence. And that's God, and we become attuned to that."[1] But is this presence really God? Based on the criteria put forth in the previous chapter, it may not be God they are attuned to at all but rather the "dynamic presence" of familiar spirits. The problem with addressing this issue is the proponents of these practices are devout and virtuous, which highly impresses a great many Christians.

With this in mind I fully realize any critical approach to these writers must be very sensitive. It is my intention to show civility and grace on this issue and not be hateful toward those individuals whose teachings and practices my research demonstrates are in error. However, if my studies are correct, such errors can open a person to a realm that leads to spiritual disaster. We are continually warned in Scripture to test and prove what is or is not from God. I do not want to provoke readers into a witch-hunt but rather to godly vigilance and discernment.

These issues are of vital importance! I personally know of people who, in the context of wanting to explore Christianity at a deeper level, have become full-blown New Agers by reading and practicing what some of the following authors have promoted. There may be some good in what these writers say, but it is also true that a little leaven can indeed leaven the whole lump (Galatians 5:9). What I am saying may appear controversial, but please keep in mind what New Age writer Marilyn Ferguson discovered: 31 percent of New Agers she quizzed said it was "Christian mysticism" that got them involved.[2] Now let's look at what some of these authors say.

M. Scott Peck

Over the past 15 years, on the New York Times best-seller list, one title has consistently stood out: *The Road Less Traveled,* by Dr. M. (Morgan) Scott Peck. LIFE magazine called it a "national institution" and compared its selling power to that of the Bible.[3] That may not be an overstatement considering the book has sold millions of copies and profoundly influenced tens of millions of people. The prestigious Wall Street Journal resounded that *The Road Less Traveled* was: "Brilliant in its insistence that there is no distinction between the process of achieving spiritual growth and achieving mental growth."[4]

In the self-help sections of many large bookstores, M. Scott Peck usually receives almost half a shelf devoted to his books. His influence is substantial and seems enduring. The remarkable chord that Peck has struck with so many readers is his no-nonsense approach to life's problems. He proposes that one should tackle adverse situations head on with the goals being both psychological and spiritual growth. But what does spiritual growth mean to Peck? This can be learned by the very statement he poses to his readers: "I have said that the ultimate goal of spiritual growth is for the individual to become as one with God." He then makes this bold proclamation: "It is for the individual to become totally, wholly God."[5] In familiar New Age fashion he believes "these concepts" have been promoted in the past "by Buddha, by Christ, by Lao-Tse, among many others."[6]

Many of Dr. Peck's admirers would be highly offended by seeing the much-decried title *New Age* in association with his name. Some may say: "Well, he was a Buddhist when he wrote the book but now he is a Christian; besides, there are so many useful ideas in that book that don't conflict with Christianity." However, to get an idea of the kind of "Christianity" Peck has espoused, from the time of his baptism on March 9, 1980 to the present consider the following facts:

Fact: In an interview with *New Age* magazine, Peck revealed that *The Road Less Traveled* was dropped on him from God, and that there are "an enormous number of people who have a passion for God, but who are fed up to the gills with fundamentalism." The interviewer also divulged that Peck moved from "Eastern mystical religions toward Christian mysticism [contemplative prayer]."[7]

Fact: Mystical prayer is also the basis for Peck's spirituality. He noted the necessity of it in his book, *A World Waiting To Be Born*: "This process of emptying the mind is of such importance it will continue to be a significant theme ... It may help to remember, therefore, that the purpose of emptying the mind is not ultimately to have nothing there; rather it is to make room in the mind for something new, something unexpected, to come in. What is this something new? It is the voice of God."[8] Peck also conveys the notion that Jesus was "an example of the Western mystic" who "integrated himself with God."[9] He added that Jesus' message to us was to "cease clinging to our lesser selves" and find "our greater true selves."[10] Contemplative prayer, he believes, "is a lifestyle dedicated to maximum awareness."[11] You might be interested to know that former Vice President Al Gore has his endorsement on the book's back cover. He praises it as being "extremely important" and an "invaluable guide," stating the book's teachings have given us "powerful new reasons for hope."[12]

Fact: *The Coming of the Cosmic Christ*, is a book in which author Matthew Fox puts forth the idea that "mysticism" should become the praxis around which all the world's religions can unite—something he calls "deep ecumenism." The "cosmic Christ," Fox explains, is the "I AM in every creature" and Jesus was someone "who shows us how to embrace our own divinity."[13] Peck thoroughly endorses Fox's statements with his comment on the back cover, that Fox is offering "...values and practice required for planetary salvation."[14] This praise is revealing since Fox advocates there should be a "shift away from the historical Jesus" and more attention given to the "cosmic Christ."[15] I am certain Peck would not give such an endorsement to a manuscript he had not read or did not totally agree with.

Perhaps the best source for finding Scott Peck's spiritual mindset is an audiocassette entitled: *Further Along The Road Less Traveled.* Peck gives a lecture of his personal views on the New Age movement. In it he reveals:

- "I spent 20 years in Zen Buddhism which prepared me for Christianity."[16]
- "Zen Buddhism should be taught in every 5th grade class in

America."[17]

- "Christianity's greatest sin is to think that other religions are not saved."[18]
- "The New Age movement can get flaky but is potentially very [g]odly and that its virtues are absolutely enormous."[19]
- "If the New Age can reform society rather than just adversely challenge it then it can be extremely holy and desperately needed."[20]
- He himself presents the question to his audience: "Is Scott Peck a New Ager?" and then answers "yes" and adds that he is "proud to be listed as an Aquarian Conspirator."[21]
- He says his Foundation For Community Encouragement is "very much a New Age organization."[22]

It is not surprising then, that in his book about the New Age movement, *Heaven on Earth*, secular journalist Michael D' Antonio saw Scott Peck as "...becoming the Billy Graham of the New Age" and that he was "a major New Age leader."[23]

Thomas Merton

What Martin Luther King was to the civil rights movement and what Henry Ford was to the automobile, Thomas Merton is to contemplative prayer. Although this prayer movement existed centuries before he came along, Merton took it out of its monastic setting and made it available to and popular with the masses. It is interesting to me that many people still think celebrity star Shirley MacLaine was the greatest influence in the New Age. But for me, hands down, Thomas Merton has influenced New Age thinking more than any person of recent decades.

Merton penned one of the most classic descriptions of New Age spirituality I have ever come across. He explained:

> It is a glorious destiny to be a member of the human race, ... now I realize *what we all are*.... If only

they [people] could all see themselves as they really
are ... I suppose the big problem would be that we
would fall down and *worship each other* ...At the center of our being is a point of nothingness which is
untouched by sin and by illusions, a point of pure
truth ... This little point ... is the pure *glory of God*
in us. It is in everybody (emphasis mine). [24]

Notice how similar Merton's description is to the occultic definition of the higher self.

Merton's description of spirituality directly corresponds with
Shirley MacLaine's and all other New Agers' views of spiritual
reality. MacLaine was more of an '80s fad (subject to late-night
television mockery and whose influence lasted only a few years)
and then dissipated. Merton, on the other hand, has had the polar-
opposite effect. He has been referred to as "the twentieth century's
most important spiritual writer."[25] In addition, a major Catholic
resource publication praised Merton, saying: "If U.S. Catholics have
a spiritual director it is Thomas Merton."[26] While many made fun
of Shirley MacLaine, Merton received high praise and widespread
respect.

After saying this, I can just hear the boisterous laughter of
outrage: "He dares to compare a man like Thomas Merton with
someone like Shirley MacLaine!" Many evangelicals think Thomas
Merton was an exceptional Christian while they view MacLaine as
a flake and a pagan. However, as I stated previously, when you
evaluate Merton's mystical worldview, it clearly echoes with what
would be considered traditional New Age thought. This is an inescapable fact!

In order to understand Merton's connection to mystical occultism, we need first to understand a sect of the Muslim world.
The Sufis are the mystics of Islam. They chant the name of Allah
as a mantra, go into meditative trances and experience *God in everything*. A prominent Catholic audiotape company now promotes a
series of cassettes Merton did on Sufism. It explains: "Merton

loved and shared a deep spiritual kinship with the Sufis, the spiritual teachers and mystics of Islam. Here he shares their profound spirituality ..."[27]

In a letter to a Sufi Master, Merton disclosed: "My prayer tends very much to what you call fana."[28] So what is fana? *The Dictionary of Mysticism and the Occult* defines it as: "The act of merging with the Divine Oneness."[29] Shirley MacLaine in her book, *Going Within*, defined her spirituality in such a way:

> Coming into alignment with my Higher Self caused and expanded self-awareness in me, which automatically led me to an expanded awareness and a gentler understanding of others. At the same time, touching my Higher Self created a sense of being aligned with the *universal spirit*, so that I felt a keener understanding of the concept that *we are all one.* (emphasis mine)[30]

Consequently, like MacLaine, Merton's mystical experiences ultimately made him a kindred spirit and co-mystic with those in Eastern religions because his insights were identical to their insights. At an interfaith conference in Thailand he encouraged:

> I believe that by openness to Buddhism, to Hinduism, and to these great Asian [mystical] traditions, we stand a wonderful chance of learning more about the potentiality of our own Christian traditions ...[31]

Please understand that contemplative prayer *alone* was the catalyst for such theological views. One of Merton's biographers made this very clear when he explained:

> If one wants to understand Merton's going to the East it is important to understand that it was his rootedness in his own faith tradition [Catholicism] that gave him the spiritual equipment [contem-

plative prayer] he needed to grasp the way of wisdom that is proper to the East .[32]

This was the ripe fruit of the desert fathers. When you borrow methods from Eastern religion you get their understanding of God. There is no other way to put it. It does not take being a scholar to see the logic of this.

Merton's influence is very strong in the Catholic church and mainline Protestant denominations, and it is starting to grow in evangelical circles. While many Christians are impressed with Merton's humility, social consciousness and piety, his intellectual dynamism is also a powerful draw. But sadly, all of Merton's qualities are neutralized by his heresies. He revealed the true state of his soul to a fellow monk prior to his trip to Thailand where his life ended by accidental electrocution. Before he left, he confided to his friend: "I am going home ... to the home I have never been in this body."[33] I do not believe Merton was talking about a premonition of his death but rather was professing the East to be his true spiritual home.

This is not a reckless assertion. Virtually all Merton scholars and biographers make similar observations. One Merton devotee wrote: "The major corpus [body] of his writings are embedded in the central idea, experience and vision of the Asian wisdom."[34]

Henri Nouwen

An individual who is fast gaining popularity and respect in Christian circles, akin to that of Thomas Merton, is the now deceased Catholic theologian Henri Nouwen. Like Merton, Nouwen combines a strong devotion to God with a poetic, comforting, yet distinctly intellectual style that hits a very strong chord with what you could call the Christian intelligentsia. Many pastors and professors are greatly attracted to his deep thinking. In fact, one of his biographers revealed that in a 1994 survey of 3,400 U.S. Protestant church leaders, Nouwen ranked second only to Billy Graham in influence among them.[35]

Nouwen also attracts many lay people who regard him as very inspirational. One person told me that Nouwen's appeal could be compared to that of motherhood—a warm comforting embrace that leaves you feeling good. Despite these glowing attributes, there are several aspects of Nouwen's spirituality that earn him a place in this book. Like Merton, Nouwen is a blend of an impressive piety going down a path that cannot be supported Biblically.

Unfortunately, this widely read and highly respected author, at the end of his life, stated in clear terms that he approached God from a universalistic view. He acknowledged:

> Today I personally believe that while Jesus came to open the door to God's house, all human beings can walk through that door, whether they know about Jesus or not. Today I see it as my call to help every person claim his or her own way to God.[36]

Nouwen's endorsement of a book by Hindu spiritual teacher Eknath Easwaran, teaching mantra meditation, further illustrates his universalist views. On the back cover, Nouwen stated: "This book has helped me a great deal."[37]

Nouwen also wrote the forward to a book that mixes Christianity with Hindu spirituality, in which he says:

> [T]he author shows a wonderful openness to the gifts of Buddhism, Hinduism and Moslem religion. He discovers their great wisdom for the spiritual life of the Christian ... Ryan [the author] went to India to learn from spiritual traditions other than his own. He brought home many treasures and offers them to us in the book.[38]

Nouwen apparently took these approaches seriously himself. In his book, *The Way of the Heart*, he advised his readers:

The quiet repetition of a single word can help us to
descend with the mind into the heart ... This way
of simple prayer ... opens us to God's active presence.[39]

But what God's "active presence" taught him, unfortunately,
stood more in line with classic Hinduism than classic evangelical
Christianity. He wrote:

Prayer is "soul work" because our souls are those
sacred centers where *all is one*, ... It is in the heart
of God that we can come to the full realization of
the *unity of all that is*. (emphasis mine)[40]

It is critical to note here that Nouwen did not say all Christians are
one; he said "all is one", which is the fundamental panentheistic concept of God—the God in everything unites everything (i.e., God is the
all in all). Like Thomas Merton, it was Nouwen's intent to make mystical prayer a pervasive paradigm within all traditions of Christianity.
He felt the evangelical church had many admirable qualities but lacked
one vital one: mysticism. He sought to remedy this by imploring: "It is
to this silence [contemplative prayer] that we all are called."[41]

Thomas Keating/Basil Pennington

In the book *Finding Grace at the Center*, written by these two Catholic
monks, the following advice is given:

We should not hesitate to take the fruit of the age-
old wisdom of the East and "capture" it for Christ.
Indeed, those of us who are in ministry should make
the necessary effort to acquaint ourselves with as
many of these Eastern techniques as possible ...

Many Christians who take their prayer life seriously

have been greatly helped by Yoga, Zen, TM and similar practices, especially where they have been initiated by reliable teachers and have a solidly developed Christian faith to find inner form and meaning to the resulting experiences.[42]

Thomas Keating and Basil Pennington have taken their Christianity and blended it with Eastern mysticism through a contemplative method they call *centering prayer.*

I met a woman who once enthusiastically told me that in her church "we use a mantra to get in touch with God." She was referring to centering prayer. It is quite accurate to say centering prayer groups are flourishing today. Moreover, many times those who embrace it are the most active and creative people in the congregation. Christian peers often see these advocates as bringing a new vitality to the church.

Keating and Pennington have both authored a number of influential books on contemplative prayer thus advancing this movement greatly. Pennington essentially wrote a treatise on the subject called *Centering Prayer* while Keating has written the popular and influential classic, *Open Mind, Open Heart,* and both are major evangelists for contemplative prayer. Keating preaches: "God's first language is Silence."[43] He taught 31,000 people in 1991 alone how to "listen to God."[44] Often hundreds of people in a single seminar will be taught how to "center."

Gerald May

An individual who has had a particularly large influence in the Christian 12-step field is psychiatrist and author Gerald May. May is also the cofounder and teacher at the Shalem Prayer Institute in Washington D.C.—one of the bastions of contemplative prayer in this country. Again, as with the other proponents named in this chapter, one finds a direct affinity between Eastern mysticism and May.

In the front of his book, *Simply Sane,* he states upfront: "The lineage of searching expressed herein arises from scriptures of the world's great religions…" He then gives thanks to two Tibetan Buddhist lamas (holy men) and a Japanese zen Master for their "particular impact" on him.[45]

The influence of Eastern spirituality is also depicted in his book, *Addiction and Grace*, which is considered to be a classic in the field of Christian recovery. In this book, May conveys that "our core … one's own center … is where we realize our essential unity with one another with all God's creation."[46]

Of course the method for entering this "core" is the silence which May makes obvious when he explains: "I am not speaking here of meditation that involves guided imagery or scriptural reflections, but of a more contemplative practice in which one just sits still and stays awake with God."[47] May is even more upfront about his Eastern metaphysical views in his book, *The Awakened Heart*, where he expounds on the "cosmic presence" which he explains is "pervading ourselves and all creation."[48]

One might defend May by saying he is just speaking of God upholding everything by His omnipresence, a clear Christian viewpoint. But May is firmly in the mystical panentheistic camp. There can be no mistaking his theological underpinnings when May reveals his meaning of "cosmic presence" in such statements as, "It is revealed in the Hindu greetings jai bhagwan and namaste that reverence the divinity that both resides within and embraces us all."[49]

Morton Kelsey

Morton Kelsey is an Episcopal priest and a popular writer among certain Christian thinkers. His most influential book, *Other Side of Silence: The Guide to Christian Meditation* has influenced tens of thousands. One publication stated that his book, *Companions on The Inner Way: The Art of Spiritual Guidance* was a "favorite among spiritual directors."[50] Where contemplative prayer has lead Kelsey is apparent in his pronouncement that: "You can find most of the New Age practices in the depth of Christianity" …"I believe that the Holy One lives in every soul."[51]

Kelsey had a close relationship with author Agnes Sanford, a renowned panentheist who wrote *The Healing Light*. Sanford in turn has influenced a number of authors who have had an impact in Christian circles.

John Main

John Main was a Benedictine monk who popularized a contemplative prayer form known appropriately enough as "the way of the mantra," which was first taught to him by a Hindu monk.[52] Since his death in 1982 a vast network of *mantric* prayer groups have sprung up in scores of countries around the world. Father Laurence Freeman has been active in spreading Main's teaching.

It is absolutely astounding to me that so many have completely ignored the source of Main's practices. The view that what works for the Hindu can work for the Christian illustrates beyond measure that the mindset of the desert fathers still thrives today.

As with all the authors I profile in this chapter, Main's name in a bibliography or suggested reading list is a good way to discover a writer's contemplative proclivities.

Matthew Fox

The individual most often spoken of as being the proponent of New Age mysticism within Christianity is writer and Episcopal priest Matthew Fox. His popular books, *Original Blessing* and *The Coming of the Cosmic Christ*, are primers for what he calls "creation-centered spirituality" which is nothing more than simple panentheism with an elegant title.

Fox has a sizable following in both Catholic and mainline Protestant circles although he has not generated near the enthusiasm or respect of Thomas Merton or Henri Nouwen. Yet Fox manifests the same God-in-everything view and aligns with Eastern religion as Merton and Nouwen did.

Although Fox began his ministries in the Catholic church before switching to the Episcopal church, he still commands considerable influence among Catholic contemplatives. He is also a popular speaker at New Age conferences.

Sitting at the Wrong Table

There are scores of similar authors and teachers of contemplative prayer but it would be redundant to profile them all. Basically, these authors echo Thomas Merton. All one really has to do is understand Merton and you understand the whole movement. It is also essential to understand that although Merton and his proponents have an impressive devotion to God and a strong commitment to moral integrity, they have married Biblical principles to a mysticism that is, through the desert fathers, derived from Eastern religions.

At this point, we must return to what the apostle Paul said: "You cannot sit at the table of the Lord and the table of demons [pagan mysticism]" (I Cor. 10:21). Zeal for God, in and of itself, is not the main criterion for the discovery of truth, but in reference to His Word, God Himself has proclaimed: "All scripture is given by inspiration of God and is profitable for doctrine, for reproof, for correction, for instruction in righteousness" (II Timothy 3:16).

No longer is the contemplative movement confined just to the Roman Catholic church and mainline Protestant camps. With a sincere desire to find a deeper walk with God many conservative, evangelical Christians are starting to explore and even embrace the spirituality of those individuals I have just profiled. This pursuit oddly covers the whole gamut of evangelical Christendom from charismatic to Baptist. Only the most discerning and Biblically grounded Christians seem aware of the dangers of the contemplative prayer movement. A lack of discernment or a misleading view of Scripture can open the doors to becoming a *contemplative* evangelical. The list of these evangelicals is growing, and you may be surprised who is involved in moving the evangelical church toward a new mystical paradigm.

4

Evangelical Hybrids

One afternoon in February of 1994, I visited the youth pastor of a large evangelical church in my community. I shared with him my discoveries about the New Age effect on our society—especially regarding the practical mystic element. He then confided in me that a notable Christian author and speaker would be conducting a seminar at his church the following November. He had read the man's first book, and an uneasy feeling about this author lingered. The author's name was Richard Foster. The youth pastor asked me to check out Foster to see what I could learn about him. I agreed to do so.

Although I knew the name Richard Foster, I knew little else about him. I examined a copy of his popular book, *Celebration of Discipline* and discovered eleven references to Thomas Merton in its bibliography. Immediately, I suspected a connection. This would not have surprised me if I had read Foster's words in the book beforehand: "[W]e should all without shame enroll as apprentices in the school of contemplative prayer."[1]

I feared Foster would promote contemplative prayer during his talk at the upcoming conference, resulting in numerous attendees seeking out a local contemplative prayer center. Alarmed, the youth pastor and I made an appointment with the senior pastor and two other staff members to express our concerns and show them some examples of what the contemplative prayer movement taught. They listened readily, and the senior pastor said he planned to discuss these issues personally with Foster in a phone conversation.

Later, after that conversation took place, the senior pastor came away from it feeling fully satisfied nothing was erroneous about Foster's agenda. Foster told him *Christian* mystics who were not schooled in the East developed the contemplative tradition. Foster also acknowledged some individuals in this movement had crossed over into Eastern thought, and Thomas Merton had been *shaped* by these ideas. Foster admitted he did not know exactly where Merton stood theologically when he died but believed we could still learn from him without *going in all the directions he went.* After this exchange, the senior pastor ended all discussion with us on the matter—Foster was coming!

In-Depth

Once I recognized Foster had passed the test before a sharp senior pastor, I began to study his teachings. I discovered he was the founder and head of an organization called Renovare, from the Latin word meaning *renewal.* The goal of this group, as stated in their material, is to provide the evangelical church with a "practical strategy" for growing spiritually. "An army without a plan will be defeated,"[2] states one of Renovare's promotional materials. Renovare provides that plan or as they refer to it: "practical training for transformed living."[3]

For the next eight months I studied Foster's work, focusing on his promotion of contemplative prayer. Foster became a riddle; his statement of faith and other writings seem clearly evangelical in nature, making it understandable why he has struck a chord with so many learned Christian readers. On the other hand, he also avidly endorses a practice that leads to a mystical panentheistic understanding of God.

For example, Foster openly quotes Merton on the virtues and benefits of contemplative prayer putting forth the view that through it God "offers you an understanding and light which are like nothing you ever found in books or heard in sermons."[4] But when one digs deeper and finds what exactly this "understanding" is, it casts a very dubious light on Foster's judgment. Listen to a few statements from some of the mystics whom Foster sees as examples of contemplative spirituality:

- "[T]he soul of the human family is the Holy Spirit."
  —Basil Pennington[5]
- "I saw that God is in all things."—Julian of Norwich[6]
- "My beloved [God] is the high mountains, and the lovely valley forests, unexplored islands, rushing rivers . . ."
  —John of the Cross[7]
- "Here [the contemplative state] everything is God. God is everywhere and in all things."— Madam Guyon[8]

The point is this: *their* silence and Foster's silence are identical, as he makes clear. By using them as models, Foster tells us to *follow them* because they have experienced *deep union with God*—and if you also want this, you must go into their silence.

But if this is the case, then Foster's use of these mystics brings up a difficult problem for him. Panentheism was the fruit of their mysticism. This mysticism led them to believe as they did, and Foster cannot distance himself from that fact. Consequently, to promote them as the champions of contemplative prayer, he is also, wittingly or not, endorsing their panentheism. What he endorses is a package. You can accept both or reject both, but you cannot have one without the other.

To clear these mystics of fundamental theological error, Foster has to also defend panentheism. Therefore the evangelical church must come to a firm consensus on panentheistic mysticism. Contemplative prayer and panentheism go together like a hand in a glove—to promote one is to promote both. *They are inseparable!* Further, when one looks at Foster's method of entering this silence, it puts his teachings in a very questionable light.

When Foster speaks of the *silence*, he does not mean external silence. In his book, *Prayer: Finding the Heart's True Home*, Foster recommends the practice of breath prayer[9]—picking a single word or short phrase and repeating it in conjunction with the breath. This is typical contemplative mysticism. In the original 1978 edition of *Cel-*

ebration of Discipline, he makes his objective clear when he states: "Christian meditation is an attempt to empty the mind in order to fill it."[10]

In *Prayer: Finding the Heart's True Home*, he ties in a quote by one mystic who advised: "You must bind the mind with one thought."[11]

This advice recalls Anthony de Mello's remarks in his contemplative prayer classic, *Sadhana: A Way to God*. His approach was virtually identical to Foster's:

> To silence the mind is an extremely difficult task. How hard it is to keep the mind from thinking, thinking, thinking, forever thinking, forever producing thoughts in a never ending stream. Our Hindu masters in India have a saying: one thorn is removed by another. By this they mean that you will be wise to use one thought to rid yourself of all the other thoughts that crowd into your mind. One thought, one image, one phrase or sentence or word that your mind can be made to fasten on.[12]

I once related Foster's *breath prayer* method to an ex-New Ager who is now a Christian. She affirmed this connection when she remarked with astonishment: "That's what I did when I was into ashtanga yoga!"

The goal of prayer should not be to *bind the mind* with a word or phrase in order to induce a mystical trance but rather to use the mind to glory in the grace of God. This was the apostle Paul's counsel to the various churches: "study to show thyself approved" (II Tim. 2:15 KJV) and "pray always" (II Thessalonians 1:11 KJV) as in talking to God with your mind and your heart.

What Foster presents, focuses not on one subject but on one *thought*. Prayer is a sequence of thoughts on a spiritual subject. Keeping the mind riveted on only one thought is unnatural and adverse to true reflection and prayer. Simple logic tells us the repeating of words has no rational value. For instance, if someone called you on the phone and just said your name or one phrase over and over, would that be something you found edifying? Of course not; you would hang up on him. Why would God feel otherwise?

The Seminar

With my new understanding of Foster, I attended the seminar in November to witness his public speaking on these issues. Foster seemed charming, winsome and gifted in speech. His oratorical skills reminded me of a Shakespearean actor on stage. His program mixed serious oratory, music, and humor in just the right doses. However, his message conveyed that today's Christians suffer from spiritual stagnation, and consequently need something more. The following are a few examples:

- "There is a hunger ..."
- "We have become barren within ..."
- "We are floundering ..."
- "People are trying rather than training."

Foster alluded to a remedy for this problem with such statements as:

- "We need a way of moving forward ..."
- "We need a plan to implement the Great Commission ..."
- "We need a simple mechanism ..."
- "This might be new or frightening but you are being drawn."[13]

After the seminar ended, curious about what he meant by these statements, I approached Foster and politely asked him, "What do you think of the current Catholic contemplative prayer movement?" He appeared visibly uncomfortable with the question and at first seemed evasive and vague.

He then replied: "Well, I don't know, some good, some bad (mentioning Matthew Fox as an example of the bad)." In defense, he said: "My critics don't understand there is this tradition within

Christianity that goes back centuries." He then said something that has echoed in my mind ever since that day. He emphatically stated, "Well, Thomas Merton tried to awaken God's people!" I realized then Foster had waded deep into Merton's belief system.

This statement regarding Merton seemed paradoxical because earlier that morning Foster made a concerted effort to convince the audience he himself most certainly had no New Age sympathies. He told the 650 people assembled that he taught people to "hear the voice of Jehovah" and not the "loose, nutty kind of a thing" of the New Age.[14] But it is precisely this alignment with Merton that undermines Foster's claim to being mystically attuned to the God of the Bible. Merton expressed views such as: "I see no contradiction between Buddhism and Christianity ... I intend to become as good a Buddhist as I can."[15]

It is essential to really understand *why* Merton said things like this in order to understand why the contemplative prayer movement presents such a potential danger to evangelical Christian churches. Merton's conversion was spiritual, not social or political, as clearly revealed in one of his biographies: "His [Merton's] change of mind with regard to the higher religions was not the result of tedious comparison and contrast or even concerted analysis. It was an outgrowth of his experience with the Absolute [God]."[16]

In other words, he found Buddhist enlightenment in contemplative prayer.

Foster has written of Merton's mystical prayer in sparkling terms. He says of Merton: "Thomas Merton has perhaps done more than any other twentieth-century figure to make the life of prayer widely known and understood."[17] Foster considers Merton's book, *Contemplative Prayer*, "a must book".[18] He also states, "Merton continues to inspire countless men and women,"[19] and credits his books as being filled with "priceless wisdom for all Christians who long to go deeper in the spiritual life."[20]

This is the same Merton who " ... quaffed [drank] eagerly from the Buddhist cup in his journey to the East."[21] Yet how could Merton be a co-mystic with Eastern religions, and Foster engage in the same method as Merton, and come out on the opposite end of the spectrum? The answer may lie in some of the places I have found Foster's books being offered.

During a trip across the country I stopped to research at the world headquarters for the Unity School of Christianity, a New Age metaphysical church located in the suburbs of Kansas City, Missouri. In their bookstore under *authors A-Z* (a who's who of New Age writers) I found no less than *five* of Foster's titles. A number of New Age bookstores also carry his books, under the headings of *mysticism*.

After seeing *Celebration of Discipline* at one New Age bookstore (a store operated by devotees of a famous Hindu swami), I asked the store's book buyer what he thought of Foster. "He is wonderful," the man gleefully replied. "His views on prayer are absolutely wonderful." I then asked if he knew Foster was considered a conservative Christian in many circles. His reply was intriguing: "Well, if he was a fundamentalist he wouldn't be sold at a bookstore like this one." He ended the conversation with further praise of Foster.

Perhaps the most unsettling example of all is in a book entitled, *The Miracle of Prayer*. This book could not be any more blatantly New Age in viewpoint, filled with occult concepts and references. Yet under suggested reading, in the back of the book, Foster's book, *Prayer: Finding the Heart's True Home* is recommended.[22]

Why do these obvious New Agers sell and promote Foster's books? The answer is unmistakable: the silence! New Agers recognize their form of prayer when they see it. They know where the silence leads. They *know* what Foster means when he advises: "Every distraction of the body, mind, and spirit must be put into a kind of suspended animation before this deep work of God upon the soul can occur."[23]

If Foster heard the "voice of Jehovah," as he claims, would God not have placed a warning upon his heart and mind that Merton taught harmful theology and not to champion him? This is a valid question.

Although Foster may be sincere and well meaning, he has unfortunately drawn on a tradition the Bible does not present or endorse. When he made an appeal from Scripture to support the credence of the contemplative prayer practice all he could find was Psalm 62:1, a verse that refers to being still and attentive to God. But this passage is certainly not suggesting that one go *beyond thought* by a sacred word or focusing on the breath. If that were the case it would be taught throughout Scripture.

A Christian supporter of Foster once defended him by claiming that Foster is teaching Christians nothing more than what the apostle Paul experienced on the road to Damascus—a direct experience of God's presence. This may sound legitimate on the surface, but if you look at certain criteria, a far different picture emerges.

First of all, as I stated in chapter two, Paul did not use a method in this situation. There was no *prayer word* or *breath prayer* that propelled him into God's presence; it was a spontaneous action of God. Paul did nothing to bring on his experience. If he had, it certainly would have been referenced in the text as an important catalyst.

Secondly (and most importantly), Paul never wrote of a method in his letters to the various churches. He spoke of various spiritual gifts, but these were not based on any sort of technique that was taught. These gifts were bestowed by God as He saw fit. On that account, Foster can certainly back up a mystical element in the Bible, but he cannot back up *his* mysticism from the Bible. Unfortunately, he has instructed multitudes that, "God has given us the Disciplines of the spiritual life as a means of receiving his grace. The Disciplines allow us to place ourselves before God so that he can transform us."[24]

I would like to impress on anyone going in this direction, the words of Solomon who gravely warned, "Every word of God is pure; He is a shield to those who put their trust in Him. Do not add to His words, lest He rebuke you, and you be found a liar" (Proverbs 30:5-6). The apostle Paul also wrote, "For I have not shunned to declare to you the whole counsel of God" (Acts 20:27). In light of these statements, if you can find the silence (i.e., sacred words, going beyond thought) anywhere in Paul's writings to the church, I will humbly apologize to Richard Foster.

Just how influential has Foster become in Christian circles? For certain, his effect on the evangelical church cannot be overestimated. In a 1993 poll by *Christianity Today*, the magazine revealed that Foster's book, *Prayer: Finding the Heart's True Home*, was the number one most popular book with its readers.[25] Astoundingly, this is the same book that well-known New Ager Rosemary Ellen Guiley has on her suggested reading list in the back of her book, *The Miracle of Prayer*.

Christianity Today also revealed Foster's famous book, *Celebration of Discipline* as number *three* on a list of books that its readers voted having "the most significant impact on their Christian life, other than the Bible."[26] Foster beat out the likes of Oswald Chambers, John Calvin, John Bunyan and A.W. Tozer, who were also on the list. In fact, the most recent edition of *Celebration of Discipline* states on the back cover that it has sold over *one million copies* over the last twenty years. That figure is astounding when you consider it is a nonfiction how-to book on spirituality. This type of book generally appeals to only a very limited segment of Christian readership.

Without a doubt Foster has generated a vast and dedicated following in the evangelical church. Any charge that he is promoting a pseudo-Christian mysticism is bound to generate a storm of controversy. However, this issue should not be taken lightly—much is at stake here.

Brennan Manning

One person who has the potential to eclipse even Foster in influence is Brennan Manning, a former Catholic priest. He has authored such popular titles as the *Ragamuffin Gospel* and *The Signature of Jesus*. His admirers include people such as Max Lucado, Amy Grant, and Michael Card. He too has struck a serious chord in the evangelical community.

His appeal is easy to understand when one hears Manning in

person. His manner is very genuine and down-home. Many admire him for his passionate and dynamic character.

When he relates how his mother mistreated him as a young child you cannot help but feel his pain deeply. However, despite all his admirable qualities and devotional intensity, he teaches contemplative prayer as a way to God.

Manning devotes an entire chapter to contemplative prayer in his popular book, *The Signature of Jesus*. He compares traditional evangelical practice with the advantages and virtues of contemplative prayer. He gives his readers the impression they are really missing out on God's love if they ignore this method of prayer. In fact, he calls this chapter "Grabbing Aholt [a hold] of God."[27] He makes it very obvious this is "the goal of contemplative prayer."[28] In the back of *Ragamuffin Gospel*, one finds none other than M. Basil Pennington. Manning strongly supports Pennington's book, *Centering Prayer*, and states Pennington's methods will provide us with "a way of praying that leads to a deep living relationship with God."[29]

That, my friend, is the crux of the matter. Does contemplative prayer lead to a deeper life with God? Did it for Pennington? Does it for Manning? Many think, perhaps, that Manning has the right answer to this question. Popular Christian author and editor-at-large of *Christianity Today*, Philip Yancey, endorsed Manning to all his own readers proclaiming, "I consider Brennan Manning my spiritual director in the school of grace."[30]

Grabbing Aholt of Who

Taking a closer look at "Grabbing Aholt of God," one comes eyeball to eyeball with none other than Thomas Merton. There is a quote from Merton's good friend, David Steidl-Rast, three from John Main (*way of the mantra*), a very revealing one from Merton himself and the following one from Merton's biographer, William Shannon:

> During a conference on contemplative prayer, the
> question was put to Thomas Merton: "How can
> we best help people to attain union with God?"
> His answer was very clear: "We must tell them that
> they are already united with God." Contemplative
> prayer is nothing other than coming into conscious-
> ness of what is already there.[31]

Merton was making reference here to his pure glory-of-God-in-everybody worldview. He is not just speaking of Christians. His universalism elsewhere repudiates that fact. Therein lies the heart of this issue when Manning invites Christians to grab "aholt" of God—it is the god of Merton they are grabbing for! But Manning is such a likeable man with such an impressive spiritual flair, few bother to look under the surface and see the true ingredients.

Behind Manning's charisma lie some troubling connections. For example, Manning favorably quotes a Catholic monk, Bede Griffiths, in two of his books, *Abba's Child* and *Ruthless Trust*. Griffiths, like Merton, "explored ways in which Eastern religions could deepen his prayer."[32] Griffiths also saw the "growing importance of Eastern religions ... bringing the church to a new vitality."[33]

Recently Manning spoke at a church in my hometown. After the meeting, I asked him about his connection with Griffiths. He told me, "I have been reading him for years going all the way back to *The Golden String*" (the autobiography of Griffiths). This book came out in 1980 so it is clear Griffiths has influenced Manning for many years. When I also asked Manning which books on prayer he liked, he recommended Thomas Keating's, *Open Mind, Open Heart*, a well known primer on the practice of centering prayer, which projects a panentheistic view of God.

Changing Trends in American Spirituality

Richard Foster and Brennan Manning both have had a widespread impact on evangelicals with their enormously popular books and seminars. In all probability, at least one copy of either author's books can be found in almost every evangelical church in America. The rise in popularity of these two authors is attributed to two major social trends that have occurred over the last twenty years.

The first trend that has captivated American spirituality is an openness to explore the formally novel or exotic—especially if couched in terms that speak to Christian devotion. A strong appeal exists for many to involve themselves in *cutting edge spirituality*. People are seeking spiritual experiences that leave behind the humdrum of dry intellectualism and stale institutionalism. These seekers are quick to jump on a bandwagon that promises spiritual refreshment and innovation.

The second trend is the *quick-fix* mentality that permeates our modern culture. People in past generations put up with life's frustrations, whereas today we see an inclination to seek out, seemingly surefire approaches that promise clear results. Our own era has nurtured a strong reliance on pragmatism. No longer is truth determined by what God has said to be true, but rather, by what works (what is practical). The question that drives many to determine truth is, "Will it make me feel good about myself?" However, for the Christian, we are not to live by what *feels good* but rather by what *is* good. We must stand by the apostle Paul's caution to the Thessalonians: "Test all things, hold fast what is good" (I Thessalonians 5:21).

Bridging the Gap

One of the most common objections by the defenders and admirers of Foster and Manning is that they are not teaching Eastern mysticism because their focus and attention is on the God of Christianity. They want people to walk more closely with Jesus Christ, not Shiva or Buddha. On the surface that is a perfectly valid defense, but if one understands a quote by the founder of the top contemplative prayer school in America, then one may see this defense is precarious at best. Tilden Edwards explained, "This mystical stream [contemplative prayer] is the Western bridge to Far Eastern spirituality."[34]

This verifies that contemplative prayer is not Eastern mysticism *per se*. But the unity of practice provides a passage into the understanding of Eastern spiritual concepts. That is why the *guilt by promotion* method is a legitimate basis for seeing who Foster and Manning regard as role-models for their practices.

For example, when Manning quotes from (and even recommends in one interview)[35] William Shannon's book, *Silence on Fire*, then one would expect to find a common ground somewhere between the two of them. Yet *Silence on Fire* contains nothing that would inspire a true evangelical. In fact, it is filled with universalist statements that would offend those with evangelical sensibilities. One portion states: "....there is a oneness in God that unites all women and men ... The goal of all true spirituality is to achieve an awareness of our oneness with God and with all of God's creation."[36]

Where is the common ground? Why does Manning see Shannon as a co-mystic? If a reasonable answer cannot be found to this question, then it must be concluded that Tilden Edwards' earlier quote is really true and that Manning may have already crossed the bridge to an Eastern spiritual understanding as did Shannon.

For Manning to have read *Silence On Fire*, he would clearly see where this practice led Shannon. So, to promote him at all, means he ignored Shannon's heresies. What makes it worse is that Shannon's heresies clearly stem from contemplative prayer and Manning *still* advocates this practice. What causes Manning to promote such people as Shannon, Griffiths, and Keating? We must look at the objectives of the "powers" and "spiritual hosts" (Ephesians 6:12) that are against the preaching of the Cross.

As Christians, we often forget that familiar spirits are fallen angels, once created to minister as messengers and to be worshipping spirits for God. They know how to be spiritually positive, and they know how to communicate God's truths. But, as the Bible states, they are on a mission to deceive "if possible, even the elect" (Mark 13:22) and come as "angel[s] of light" (II Corinthians 11:14). This explains why God has given every born again Christian the Holy Spirit and His living Word to discern what is of God and what is not. When we go beyond the teachings of Scripture (as Manning and Foster have done in their contemplative prayer advocacy) with the silence, we are, indeed, entering dangerous ground.

Dr. Rodney R. Romney, Senior Pastor of the First Baptist Church of Seattle is a person frequently quoted as an example of a New Age Christian. He very candidly revealed what was conveyed to him in his contemplative prayer periods. The "source of wisdom" he was in contact with told him the following: "I want you to preach this one-ness, to hold it up before the world as my call to unity and together-ness. In the end this witness to the oneness of all people will under-mine any barriers that presently exist."[37]

Clearly, this is a familiar spirit speaking here. Jesus Christ did not teach all people are one. There are the *saved* and the *unsaved.* And Jesus Christ is the catalyst for this partition. But the spirit who spoke to Dr. Romney also revealed something else vitally important. It declared, "Silence is that place, that environment where I work. "[38]

Please pay attention to this! God does not work in *the silence*— familiar spirits do. Moreover, what makes it so dangerous is that they are very clever. One well known New Ager revealed what his guiding (familiar) spirit candidly disclosed: "We work with all who are vibrationally sympathetic; simple and sincere people who feel our spirit moving, but for the most part, only within the context of their current belief system. "[39]

The term "vibrationally sympathetic" here means those who sus-pend thought through word repetition or breath focus—inward men-tal silence. *That* is what attracts them. *That* is their opening. *That* is why Tilden Edwards called this the "bridge to far Eastern spirituality," and this is what is being injected into the evangelical church!

In *The Signature of Jesus*, Manning teaches how to suspend thought. He instructs his readers methodically:

"The first step in faith is to stop thinking about God in prayer ... "[40] "Contemplative spirituality tends to emphasize the need for a change in consciousness ... we must come to see reality differently."[41]

"Choose a single, sacred word ... repeat the sacred word inwardly, slowly, and often."[42]

"[E]nter into the great silence of God. Alone in that silence, the noise within will subside and the Voice of Love will be heard."[43]

If one could draw a spiritual tree of both Manning's and Foster's mystical heritage it would look like this: from India to Alexandria, to the desert fathers, to Thomas Merton to them; and now, through them and others like them to you. What it *should* look like is: from the triune God to His holy prophets and apostles to you. Very simple! That, my friend, is the decisive factor of this controversy.

I am aware that Foster and Manning both say things that would stir the heart of any Christian. But the issue here is one of mysticism. Is their mysticism legitimate? Prayer is not to stop thinking about God. Prayer is to think intently on God, to direct all your thoughts toward God. There is no getting around the fact that contemplative prayer is heretical. When one reads the following quote by William Shannon quoting Merton, this conclusion is inescapable: "The contemplative experience is neither a union of separate identities nor a fusion of them; on the contrary, *separate identities disappear* in the All Who is God (emphasis mine)."[44]

In essence, he is saying there is only one big identity—God. This is more in tune with *core shamanism* than Christianity, yet Manning embraces Shannon. In Leviticus 19:31, God says "I am the Lord your God," not *we* are the Lord thy God. Only God possesses God's identity.

Other evangelicals of national profile are also embracing contemplative prayer. I did not bring their names forward because their positions are identical to Foster and Manning, and the issues would be redundant. I am not interested in slinging mud on names; rather, I am challenging the Christian community to look at the facts surrounding the contemplative prayer movement and see its connection to New Age occultism and Eastern mysticism.

Just because a writer is emotionally stirring, sincere, and uses Biblical language does not necessarily mean he or she advocates Biblical truths. A good example is Catholic devotion to Mary, the mother of Jesus. Most of those who practice this would be very likable, devout people who would have a number of Bible verses in hand to support their position. But is Mary-devotion Biblically grounded? The same principle applies to Foster and Manning. Is contemplative prayer Biblical or is it merely tradition?

For those who hold to the authoritative view of the Bible these errors can easily be seen. After one pastor became aware of the issues covered in this chapter he made the keen observation, "How can Foster and Manning receive spiritual nourishment from people who throw out the Great Commission?" He summed up in this one observation the whole controversy with the men I have just profiled. How can a Christian leader like Manning recommend Thomas Keating's book on centering prayer when Keating says things like, "In order to guide persons having this experience [divine oneness], Christian spiritual directors may need to dialogue with Eastern teachers in order to get a fuller understanding." Keating is, in effect, stating that Christian leaders must turn to Hindus and Buddhists to understand the result of centering prayer. In addition, how can Foster feel the way he does toward Thomas Merton when Merton shared a spiritual kinship with Buddhists and Sufis who have rejected the "word of reconciliation" (II Corinthians 5:19)?

These are hard questions that *need* to be answered! And if they cannot be effectively answered, then maybe we shouldn't "enroll in the school of contemplative prayer" or expect to hear the "Voice of Love" in the silence.

5

Discernment

A Christian mom whom I know had been researching the New Age for some time and felt she must share the information with others. She recognized how New Age thought had saturated our society and wanting to alert others, she organized a seminar series at her church. After the seminars, many people approached her to say thanks for a job well done. However, some of the parents were unconcerned and told her they did not have to worry about such things because they did not yet "have children of high school age."

This naive response is all too common among evangelicals today. When they hear the term New Age many tend to equate it with wayward teens dabbling in ouija boards or astrology. We certainly have our children to be concerned about. Nevertheless, it is often middle-aged Christians who are open to the *upscale* side of metaphysics and incredibly enough, some of the most intelligent and well-read people show the most interest.

A vast number of Christians feel they are invulnerable to being mislead, simply because they are adults. This is not the case at all. Considering today's spiritual and social climate, adults need discernment as much or more than teens. As we move closer to the return of Christ, Scripture makes clear reference to the spirits of delusion that will manifest themselves with increased effectiveness.

The Chicken Soup Phenomenon

In recent years, a series of high profile, immensely successful books (80 million sold) have had an impact on the lives of many Christians. They are the *Chicken Soup for the Soul* books by Jack Canfield and Mark Victor Hansen. Although these books are filled with charming and uplifting stories, Canfield's spirituality is quite disturbing from a Christian viewpoint. In understanding the foundational views of these two authors, one must ask, "Can a corrupt tree bring forth good fruit" (Luke 6:43)?

A New Age magazine article from 1981 revealed Canfield was no less than a teacher of the highly occultic "psychosynthesis" method developed by a direct disciple of Alice Bailey (see Bailey's clear occultism and birthing of the term *New Age* in chapter two). From some of his most recent writings, Canfield openly reveals he had his "spiritual awakening" in a yoga class in college where he felt God "flowing" through all things.[1] Hence, Canfield also promotes many occult writers.

In order to draw a conclusion on the spiritual persuasions of the *Chicken Soup For The Soul* authors take a look at one particular book they both enthusiastically endorse. The book is called *Hot Chocolate for the Mystical Soul*, compiled by Arielle Ford. It is the identical format of the *Chicken Soup For The Soul* series—101 stories by different authors on a particular theme.

Ford's book permeates with Eastern and New Age metaphysical content. A panoply of psychics, mediums, astrologers, channelers and especially Hindu mystics present an array of stories. One such story is about a psychic who writes of her abilities.[2]

Another story in the book is about a Hindu holy man who manifests "holy ash" out of thin air.[3] Yet another involves a man who claims to be the reincarnation of the apostle Paul and writes that the message of Jesus is "God dwells within each one of us [all humanity]."[4]

Co-author of the *Chicken Soup For The Soul* series, Mark Victor

Hansen, agreed with Ford's book so deeply that he wrote the fore-word. A few excerpts from this foreword reveal Hansen's view that these "enlightening stories will inspire you. They will expand your awareness, ... you will think in new exciting and different ways ... You will be renewed through the tools, techniques and strategies contained herein ... May your mystical soul be united with the mystical magical tour you've been wanting and waiting for."[5]

Jack Canfield echoed this praise on the back cover by stating, "They [the stories in the book] will change your beliefs, stretch your mind, open your heart and expand your consciousness."[6]

The key words in these endorsements are—"change your beliefs," "expand your awareness," "think in new ways." It is apparent the underlying theme of Canfield and Hansen's comments are the advocation of moving people towards New Age mysticism. This should be alarming to Christians in light of the popularity of these authors. Someone who loves the *Chicken Soup For The Soul* series and reads these endorsements may buy Ford's book thinking it must be spiritually sound since the series has such good stories. They may read the accounts of Eastern meditation and buy into it because they think so highly of Canfield and Hansen.

Canfield endorses an even more intriguing book entitled *Nurturing Spirituality In Children*. This metaphysical book is a virtual *how-to* handbook on introducing a child to his/her higher self. The author states, "It is our duty to turn them within to their Inner Teacher ..."[7] Further, the book is filled with affirmations that children should repeat: "I am one with Spirit, or God," and "I allow the energy of Spirit to flow through me."[8] On the front cover of this book, Canfield enthusiastically endorses this approach with the beaming pronouncement, "Indispensable in developing children's self-esteem and a balanced life."[9]

Jack Canfield is supposedly coming out with a book entitled *Chicken Soup for the Conscious Soul*. His plans to donate part of the profits of this book to the well-known New Age Omega Center in upstate New York are a clear indication of Canfield's intent for this book.[10]

These books are selling like hotcakes in some evangelical bookstores because they are *positive*. If someone would have told me fourteen years ago that such books would be someday selling in Christian bookstores I would have said they were nuts—no way!

Sadly, other such books have seeped into Christian bookstores. In one store, Sara Ban Breathnach's book, *Simple Abundance, A Daybook of Comfort and Joy* was spotted under a sign which read, "For Devotions." In this book she informs her readers we are all "asleep to our divinity."[11] Yet, in spite of her obvious connection to the New Age, I have been told that women's prayer groups at evangelical churches have ordered this book in bulk!

Creeping Metaphysics

If you are wondering at this point why these authors and their teachings are *creeping* by many Christians, then maybe the definition of *creeping* might help. The term means: slowly advancing at a speed that is not really apparent until you look back over a long time period. For instance, creeping inflation is not noticed in the short term, but when one looks back over 20-30 years it is shocking. A meal that cost two dollars in 1970 now may cost eight dollars—however, the increase moved so slowly that the impact was diminished.

This is the same kind of movement we have been seeing with the New Age within our society. Metaphysical New Ageism is gradually becoming mainstream. What was once seen as flaky is now normal today—even useful. This trend is impacting evangelical Christianity at only a slightly lesser degree than secular society. The reason for only the slight variance is because many, perhaps most Christians, have not yet grasped the *practical mystic* approach that New Age proponents have adapted themselves to.

This mystical pragmatism is growing particularly fast through various New Age healing techniques. One such procedure is called Reiki (pronounced ray-key), a Japanese word that translates *universal life energy* or *God energy*. It has also been referred to as the *Radiance Technique*. Reiki is an ancient Tibetan Buddhist healing system, redis-covered by a Japanese man in the 1800s and only recently has come to the West.

The Reiki technique consists of placing the hands on the re-cipient and then activating the energy to flow through the practi-tioner and into the recipient. One practitioner described the expe-rience in the following way:

> When doing it, I become a channel through which this force, this juice of the universe, comes pouring from my palms into the body of the person I am touching, sometimes lightly, almost imperceptibly, sometimes in famished sucking drafts. I get it even as I'm giving it. It surrounds the two of us, patient and practitioner.[12]

What is this "juice of the universe?" The answer is an impor-tant one, and was answered by a renowned Reiki master who ex-plained:

> A Reiki attunement is an initiation into a sacred metaphysical order that has been present on earth for thousands of years ... By becoming part of this group, you will also be receiving help from the Reiki guides and other spiritual beings who are also work-ing towards these goals.[13]

While this is not widely advertised, Reiki practitioners depend on this "spirit guide" connection as an integral aspect of Reiki. In fact, it is the very basis of Reiki. One Reiki master who has enrolled hundreds of other masters spoke of her interaction with the spirit guides:

> For me, the Reiki guides make themselves the most
> felt while attunements are being passed. They stand
> behind me and direct the whole process, and I as-
> sume they also do this for every Reiki Master. When
> I pass attunements, I feel their presence strongly
> and constantly. Sometimes I can see them.[14]

A Christian's initial response to this information might be: "So what. I don't travel in those circles so it does not concern me." This undaunted viewpoint would be valid except for the fact that Reiki is currently growing to enormous proportions and in some very influential circles. (It may even be in your local hospitals, schools and youth organizations.) It is essential to know that many nurses, counselors and especially massage therapists use Reiki as a supplement to their work. It is often promoted as a *complementary* service.

Even more significant are the numbers involved in this practice. Examine the following figures to catch just a glimpse of the growing popularity of Reiki. In 1998, there were approximately 33,000 Reiki listings on the Internet. Today that number, on some search engines, exceeds *one million* listings. In just four years, there has been a 3000 percent growth on Internet listings of Reiki! And even that number is just a fraction of those who practice it. One Reiki master delightfully noted this surge of interest when he stated:

> Over the years, there has been a shift in the belief
> system of the general public, allowing for greater
> acceptance of alternative medicine. As a result, we
> are seeing a growing interest in Reiki from the pub-
> lic at large. People from all backgrounds are com-
> ing for treatment and taking classes.[15]

Another revealing statistic involves Louisville, Kentucky, where 102 people were initiated into Reiki in just a single weekend.[16] This denotes a large number of people are drawn to Reiki in the Bible belt, a traditional and conservative part of America.

The reason for this level of acceptance is easy to understand. Most people, many Christians included, believe if something is spiritually positive then it is of God. A pastor friend of mine recounted a situation in which a Christian, who had some physical problems, turned to Reiki for comfort. When this pastor advised the man that Reiki fundamentally opposed the Christian worldview he became furious and responded with the following defense: "How can you say this is bad when it helped me?" That is why I entitled this chapter "discernment." To discern is to "test the spirits" (1 John 4:1). If something is of God it will conform to the basic tenant of God's plan to show His grace through Christ Jesus and Him alone (Ephesians 2:7). Reiki, as I defined earlier, is based on the occult-view of God.

Another such method is *Therapeutic Touch*. Like Reiki, it is based on the occult *chakra* system, portrayed as the seven *energy centers* in the body aligned with spiritual forces. The seventh chakra identifies with the God-in-all view. Therapeutic Touch is widely practiced by nurses in clinics and hospitals. It is seen as a helpful and healing adjunct to nursing care.

If the connection between Reiki healing and other metaphysical practices can be seen, then we more fully understand why the following quote is one of the most powerful statements as to the true nature of contemplative prayer. A Reiki master in the course of promoting the acceptance of this method declared:

> Anyone familiar with the work of … or the thought of … [she then listed a string of notable New Age writers with Thomas Merton right in the middle of them] will find compatibility and resonance with the theory and practices of Reiki.[17]

Reiki comes from Buddhism, and as one Merton scholar wrote,

"The God he [Merton] knew in prayer was the same experience that Buddhists describe in their enlightenment."[18]

This is why it is so important to understand the connection between the writings of Foster and Manning with Merton. Promotion indicates attachment, and attachment indicates common ground. Something is terribly wrong when a Reiki master and two of the most influential figures in the evangelical church today both point to the same man as an example of their spiritual path.

Stress Reduction

Overstressed people are looking for new avenues to better health each day. Stress is believed to be one of the leading causes of illness in America today. Millions of people suffer from disorders such as headaches, insomnia, nerves, and stomach problems because of excessive tension in their lives. In response to this situation, an army of practitioners has come forward to teach *relaxation skills* and *stress-reduction techniques* to the affected millions. One newspaper article proclaimed:

> Once a practice that appealed mostly to mystics and occult followers, meditation now is reaching the USA's mainstream … The medical establishment now recognizes the value of meditation and other mind-over-body states in dealing with stress-related illness.[19]

When one compares the meditation techniques used in stress reduction and the meditation used in New Age spirituality, it is easy to see these practices as basically the same. Both methods use either the breathing technique or mantra exercises to still the mind. Unknown to most people, a blank mind in a meditative state is all that is necessary for contact with a *spirit guide*.

An example of this is John Randolph Price, founder of the Quartus Foundation and instigator of the December 31 World

Healing Day Meditation, who became involved in New Age meta-physics through just such a meditative wandering. He revealed:

> Back when I was in the business world, the American Management Association put out a little book on meditation, which indicated that meditation was a way to attain peace of mind and reduce stress in a corporate environment. So I decided I'd try it ... I discovered how to come into a new sphere of consciousness. Consciousness actually shifts, and you move into a realm you may not have even known existed.[20]

Many people have involuntarily become New Agers by simply seeking to improve their physical and mental health through meditation. Two examples on this issue are comments made by two authors who honor the higher self view of man, Joan Borysenko and Ann Wise. Borysenko, a medical doctor, stated the following revelation: "I originally took up secular meditation for its medical benefits and in time discovered its deeper psychological and spiritual benefits."[21]

Ann Wise, who works in the corporate field to improve decision-making abilities for business people, made an identical observation:

> Those who initially participate in this work purely for enhancements to their productivity in the corporate world are often startled and pleased by what one VP called "the value and inevitable focus on spirituality that evolved from the work." ... I often find that individuals who began brainwave training [meditation] for a specific, objective purpose also become quickly interested and involved in seeking higher levels of spiritual consciousness.[22]

Here lies the basic message of *A Time of Departing*. The silence is really all the same. It transcends context. Whatever the format in which it is placed, from stress reduction to contemplative prayer, it inevitably leads to a certain spiritual perception, but one that does not correspond to the Gospel of the grace of God found in Jesus Christ.

Yoga

This new spiritual awareness is often discovered in a popular practice known as yoga. This Eastern technique was so in vogue that in 1992, Newsweek magazine proclaimed, "The Boomers Turn to Yoga!"[23] The article spoke of the sharp rise of interest in this practice and the increased demand for it. By 1998, USA Weekend's supplement indicated the trend was still going strong:

> Yoga is finding itself in an unusual position these days. Finally shaking its reputation as a 1960s remnant, the body-bending practice has become a staple in some surprising circles ... Today, more than 6 million Americans practice yoga, and the numbers are growing.[24]

A prominent figure responsible for the current respectability of yoga is Dr. Dean Ornish. His program for reversing heart disease presents yoga as a key element in making a comeback from cardiac problems. Newsweek magazine says of his efforts:

> Over the past two decades, this Sausalito-based internist has pushed just as hard to revolutionize American medicine ... Forty major insurance companies now cover Ornish's program as an alternative to surgery. Medicare may soon follow suit ... "[25]

From a Christian perspective, the spiritual precepts *behind* yoga are blatantly occultic. Dr. Ornish believes (as do most yoga advocates) that "Everyone and everything is God in disguise."[26]

With a staggering *fifteen million* people in the United States alone now practicing yoga, friends, co-workers, bosses, and even many doctors are exposing a great number of Christians to it as a *health enhancer.*

Remember! Yoga has its roots in Hinduism, as the article by USA Weekend implied: "Many people use yoga's meditative nature as a path to spiritual growth ... it can actually enhance religion."[27]

Not only are baby boomers turning to mystical healing and spirituality through yoga, but their kids, the *baby busters*, have now one of their major pop icons to lead them down this path. The pop singer Madonna has emerged as an advocate of yoga. After many years of success and wealth, the material girl became confused about life. After discovering ashtanga yoga, she became an enthusiastic devotee.

Interestingly, in one of her music videos, there is a scene, which shows her meditating while surrounded by a number of lights. Philip St. Romain described this same scene in his mystical experience with the *lights*. (I shared Romain's experience in the second chapter of this book.)

Because yoga is now so deeply entrenched in the fabric of American culture, New Age spirituality will play an even larger role for society in the future. If yoga were just stretching and exercise then there would not be any concern about spiritual pitfalls. However, yoga is, in many cases, about emptying of the mind and going into a silence that has spiritual ramifications. Catholic priest Thomas Ryan notes:

> The primary aims of yoga are spiritual ... Yoga seeks
> to cultivate a focused awareness of one's deepest be-

ing, one's Self, and in that Self, God. Physical exercises are but the skin of yoga; its sinews and skel-
eton are *mental* exercises [meditation] that prepare the
way for a transformation of consciousness ... [28]

The Guru of Self-Help

Without question the most influential practical mystic today is talk
show host Oprah Winfrey. Her predominantly female audience,
numbering in the tens of millions, look to her as the source of
their spiritual inspiration—even more so than church in many cases.

I realize speaking critically of someone as warm and caring as
Oprah might stir angry emotions in many of her viewers. Nonetheless, please keep in mind that with Oprah, as with the others I
have written about, her obvious good qualities are not the issue
here. It is what she *promotes* that I challenge. Like Foster and Manning, I admire Oprah as a person, but, what she promotes is the
concern.

Somewhere during her career, Oprah read a book entitled, *Discover The Power Within You,* by Unity minister Eric Butterworth. In
line with Unity teaching the book expounded the *Divinity of Man*
as perceived through mystical practice. Oprah embraced these views
so earnestly that she advocated:

> This book changed my perspective on life and reli-
> gion. Eric Butterworth teaches that God isn't 'up
> there.' He exists inside each one of us, and it's up to
> us to seek the divine within.[29]

Her talk show has launched many New Age authors into national super-stardom—authors such as Marianne Williamson, Sa-
rah Ban Breathnach, Iyanla Vanzant, and Cheryl Richardson.

One such author propelled into prominence by Oprah, with
regard to New Age teaching, is Gary Zukav. Zukav became a

regular guest on the Oprah show following his first appearance in October of 1998. Afterwards, his book entitled *The Seat of the Soul* became a constant fixture at the top of the New York Times best-seller list for an astounding two years!

The Seat of the Soul, pure and simple, is a spiritual primer or manual for New Age thought. It has gained such popularity even though it lacks the elements that have traditionally attracted wide readership (i.e., novels, biography, scandal, health, etc.). The book's basic message is, "Dwell in the company of your nonphysical Teachers and guides [spirit guides]."[30]

The Seat of the Soul has struck a chord with an enormous number of people. The notion of "nonphysical guides and teachers" is now considered perfectly acceptable by a vast number of the reading public. When such a book is embraced by so many for so long it means the New Age is already here. Clearly, our society is not heading toward the cliff concerning New Age spirituality—we are already over it!

Dr. Phil

One of the major figures to impact the viewing masses through Oprah is Dr. Phil McGraw. In fact he has been a regular on her show every Tuesday for a very long time.

While Gary Zukav is sort of spooky and mystical, Dr. Phil is folksy and outgoing. His advice is also much more practical and common sense than Zukav.

The concern with Dr. Phil and his influence on perhaps millions of Americans is warranted because of his enormous popularity. He is perhaps the most sought after counselor/therapist in the country and has in fact recently started his own television talk show. He is heartily admired by non-Christian and Christian alike. In light of this growing acceptance and influence, it is only prudent for every discerning believer to take a closer look at Dr. Phil's message. When he first appeared on the Oprah show, I thought Dr. Phil may have been an evangelical Christian. He quotes from the Bible in one of his books and emphasizes the importance of God in one's life.

After some careful scrutiny however, I realized McGraw didn't place much emphasis on Jesus Christ. In fact, he rarely mentioned Him. In the place of Jesus Christ, Dr. Phil promotes what he calls the inner *core of consciousness* that indwells every human being. This concept resonates with similarity to the New Age higher self. And when Dr. Phil quotes, in his book *Relationship Rescue,* 19th century Transcendentalist Ralph Waldo Emerson who says, "What lies behind us and what lies in front of us pales in comparison of what lies within us," we are left only to wonder if Dr. Phil shares Emerson's panentheistic view on God and humanity. Emerson drew much of his spiritual views from the Hindu Upanajhads and believed God was within everyone, all the while maintaining an ardent opposition to the Christian gospel.

The New Age Christian—An Accepted Oxymoron

All this popularity with meditative mysticism presents a very new and perplexing challenge for evangelical Christianity. We are beginning to encounter the *New Age Christian.* This new term describes someone who remains in his or her home church and professes the Christian faith but has also incorporated various aspects of the New Age worldview into his or her life. Philosopher David Spangler was very optimistic about the possibility of this integration when he wrote, "The point is that the New Age is here ... it builds itself and forms itself in the midst of the old."[31]

What has fueled the momentum of this trend is the buffet dining approach that has marked American religious sensibilities in the last twenty years—you take what you want and leave the rest. Americans are picking and blending religions as if they were ordering espressos: pick your espresso blend, but you still get coffee—pick your spiritual path, but you still get God. Whatever suits your spiritual tastes, you bring together. The result is hybrid New

Age spirituality.

I recall a conversation once with a woman in a coffee bar. We chatted on spiritual subjects, and her comments led me to believe she was an evangelical Christian. Towards the end of our friendly conversation she dropped a bombshell on me when she blurted-out, "Well, we all have the Christ-consciousness!"

In another incident, a local pastor shared with me how a woman he had long known as a strong solid Christian was almost swept up by New Age thinking. Her young adult son had been addicted to drugs and went through a drug rehab program. In the process his counselor introduced him to New Age spirituality. He, in turn, shared it with his mother, giving her a book to read entitled *Conversations With God* (a New Age best seller).

Incredibly, she found herself being swayed by the book's arguments and began to doubt whether or not her evangelical Christianity was indeed the only way to God. Her desire to see her son aligned with God left her mind open in welcoming the possibility that various mystical paths were equally genuine in finding God. It took this pastor nearly two hours to help this women understand the error of her thinking. Keep in mind this was a strong and well-grounded Christian who had been living her Christian faith for decades. If these strong Christians can be swayed, what about people who are even more vulnerable to what is going on in the larger culture? What chance do they have in not being deceived?

The New Age message has such a positive ring that it is necessary to look behind the appealing facade to see what is *actually* there. If one goes to a massage therapist who does Reiki one should know the true nature of that practice. If your doctor wants you to meditate, you should know the spiritual dangers of non-Biblical meditation. As America moves further into a mystical society it will become increasingly difficult to escape the ideas and practices described in this chapter. Christians must become aware of what is happening in order to make informed choices about things that may affect them spiritually. In addition, many of our friends, family, co-workers, etc. will be seeking spiritual solutions to the uncertainties of our society.

Interest in this movement and its practices are accelerating to such a degree that most people will encounter this sometime or somewhere soon. One highly respected Christian counselor made the following assessment regarding the momentum of the New Age practical mystics:

> We cannot overstate how profoundly their impact is being felt in education, business, medicine, and psychotherapy. It is safe to say that the prevailing religion in America … is no longer Christianity but is instead New Age.[32]

Probably the majority of people in America has a family member or close friend who does mantra meditation, practices yoga, has encountered Reiki, Therapeutic Touch, or is an avid fan of the Oprah Winfrey show. How could anyone dare to say that any of these seemingly benign or even helpful subjects have a connection to Satan or that which is evil? A brother in Christ whom I met for coffee one day gave me the answer to that question. He referred to the very act that caused the fall of humanity, based on something that *looked* good: "So when the woman saw that the fruit of the tree was good for food, that it was pleasant to the eyes, and a tree desirable to make one wise, she took of its fruit and ate" (Genesis 3:6).

The temptation of Eve reminds us that our sin-based troubles can be traced back to something appearing to be good that was, in fact, evil.

Secondly, and just as important, what actually constitutes that which is satanic? Virtually everyone in Christendom equates that term, satanic, with things dark and sinister. However, the Bible paints a far different picture of Satan—one that fits the New Age movement perfectly. Satan said, 'I will be like the Most High" (Isaiah 14:14). He did not say he would *be* the most high; he said he would be *like* the Most High. The word "like" here means to *correspond to.*

How could Satan accomplish this mission?

Satan is not simply trying to draw people to the dark side of a good versus evil conflict. Actually, he is trying to eradicate the gap between himself and God, between good and evil, altogether. When we understand this approach it helps us see why Thomas Merton said everyone is already united with God (page 78) or why Jack Canfield said he felt God flowing through *all* things. All means all; nothing left out. Such reasoning implies that God has given His glory to all of creation; since Satan is part of creation, then he too shares in this glory, thus is "like *the Most High*."

Contrary to this New Age belief of good and evil merging and man or any part of creation becoming "like the Most High" Man and God can only be brought together through the Cross. If the all-in-one view were true, then salvation through a redemptive Savior would become unnecessary and Jesus going to the Cross rendered in vain. In order for the Cross to make any sense, there must be a separation of God's perfect nature and Man's sin nature. We know Satan has only one enemy —the Cross; he knows without it no human being can be restored to God.

The Bible says the message of the Cross is the power of God (I Cor. 1:18), and while there *are* two opposing spiritual realms, God has always and will always prevail. Satan can never thwart God's ultimate purposes. And yet, today's Western society is enticed by practical mystics who deny, by their own proclamations, God's plan of eternal salvation. Will the majority of people come to believe that all is one and there is no good and evil distinction? Such a plan now exists and will shape future events—events that will alter the course on which millions will advance.

6

Could This Really Be The End of the Age?

Throughout my Christian life I have periodically heard fellow Christians suggest we are in *the last days*. Often these comments were initiated from current cases of violent crimes, sexual perversions, war or natural disasters. Since I knew history had repeatedly encountered these calamities, such pronouncements of Christ's imminent return rang hollow.

However, in 1984 a novel and alarming occurrence raced to my attention. A friend educated me about the *New Age movement* and its end-times implications. After a period of investigation, I came to believe this could very well be the time period the book of Revelation addresses. Instead of a vague and obscure manifestation of prophecy, I saw something distinct and pervasive happening in our churches and society. And I don't believe it is just an accident. At the risk of sounding conspiratorial, it has been predicted from both sides of the struggle.

Christians must remember the authenticity of Christianity itself is predicated upon its prophecies coming to pass. Jesus Christ, the apostle Paul and many others make clear and direct references to particular events occurring in the future. If these events are only fantasies then everything else could be equally fictitious. I believe current trends authenticate the claims of Jesus Christ being who He claimed to be. Upon examination of the evidence, it becomes clear that the course our society (and our churches) is taking has been foretold by the apostolic writings.

The apostle Paul spoke of the "Day of the Lord" in reference to "the times and seasons" in the fifth chapter of I Thessalonians. He describes how God will bring change swiftly and without delay. Paul states:

> But concerning the times and the seasons, brethren, you have no need that I should write to you.
>
> For you yourselves know perfectly that the day of the Lord so comes as a thief in the night. For when they say, "Peace and safety!" then sudden destruction comes upon them, as labor pains upon a pregnant woman. And they shall not escape.
>
> But you, brethren, are not in darkness, so that this Day should overtake you as a thief. You are all sons of light and sons of the day. We are not of the night nor of the darkness. Therefore let us not sleep, as others do, but let us watch and be sober. (I Thessalonians 5:1-6)

Paul is saying the end of the age will come upon the world like a thief in the night. In other words, it will actually *sneak up* on people. Then interestingly, the apostle contrasts two groups: "But you, brethren [followers of Christ], are not in darkness [people of ignorance] so that this Day should overtake you as a thief [unaware]" (v.4). Here, Paul is saying believers in Christ will have the information available to them to prepare for "that day."

Those who walk in the light can see both where they are going and what is coming ahead. Paul then warns against spiritual slumber and drunkenness, which could lead to a person being overtaken by that day, unaware: "Therefore let us not sleep, as others do; but let us watch and be sober" (v. 6). The word sober here means *alert* or *aware*. If we are instructed to watch and be aware, there must be something to watch for—otherwise, Paul's admonition would be useless. But who and what are we to watch for?

The Coming One

In the early twentieth century, a figure who would have a major impact on the Western esoteric movement came out of the occultic Theosophical Society. The popularization of the very term *New Age* has been attributed to her writings. Her name was Alice Ann Bailey.

Born, Alice LaTrobe-Bateman, in Manchester, England on June 16, 1880, she grew up as a society girl and enjoyed all the privileges of the British upper class. Being very religious, Alice met and married a man who later became an Episcopal minister. In time, they moved to the United States. When Alice's husband physically abused her, she left him and settled with her three children in Pacific Grove, California.

Alice was greatly comforted when she met two other English women living in Pacific Grove. These women introduced her to theosophy, which seemed to provide answers to her questions concerning why such misfortune had befallen her. Alice, then 35, was about to have her life changed forever. Later, in her unfinished autobiography, she wrote:

> I discovered, first of all, that there is a great and divine Plan ... I discovered, for a second thing, that there are Those Who are responsible for the working out of that Plan and Who, step by step and stage by stage, have led mankind on down the centuries.[1]

In 1917, Alice moved to Los Angeles and began working for that plan at the Theosophical Society headquarters where she met Foster Bailey, a man who had devoted his life to occultism. She divorced her former husband and married Bailey in 1920. Alice had her first contact with a voice that claimed to be a master in

November of 1919. Calling himself the Tibetan, he wanted Alice to take dictation from him. Concerning this, Alice wrote " ... I heard a voice which said, 'There are some books, which it is desired, should be written for the public. You can write them. Will you do so?'"[2]

Alice felt reluctant at first to take on such an unusual endeavor, but the voice continued urging her to write the books. At this point in time Alice experienced a brief period of anxiety in which she feared for her health and sanity. One of her other spirit "masters" finally reassured her she had nothing to fear and she would be doing a "really valuable piece of work."[3] The "valuable work" Alice was to do ended up lasting thirty years. Between 1919 and 1949, by means of telepathic communication, Alice Bailey wrote 19 books for her unseen mentor.

To occultists, the significance of the Alice Bailey writings has heralded anticipation of the appearance of a *World Healer and Savior* in the coming Aquarian Age (the astrological age of enlightenment and peace). This savior would unite all mankind under his guidance. Bailey termed him the *Coming One*. This person was not to be the Lord Jesus Christ, whom Christians await the return of but an entirely different individual. This man is to embody all the great principles of occultism, chiefly the *divinity and perfectibility of man*. One of Bailey's followers wrote:

> The reappearance of the Avatar [world teacher], by whatever name he may be known, has been prophesied in many religions as well as in the esoteric [occult] tradition. A major manifestation is expected in connection with the Aquarian age.[4]

Interestingly, the apostle Paul declared one called "the man of sin, the son of perdition" would also proclaim himself to be *God*. I believe this coming Aquarian messiah will be the son of perdition spoken of by Paul in II Thessalonians. Furthermore, I am convinced the New Age movement is his spiritual platform. Too many things fit together for this to be just a coincidence. Therefore, we must watch for the restructuring of our world to prepare for his entry.

Daniel 8:23 states this man will be a master of dark sayings. In Hebrew, this translates as one skilled in cunning and ambiguous speech. The world will see him as one who is distinguished and spiritually brilliant. Keep this in mind as you read the following description:

> The coming one will not be Christian, a Hindu, a Buddhist, not an American, Jew, Italian or Russian— his title is not important; he is for all humanity, to unite all religions, philosophies and nations.[5]

The only one who could bring this about is the one who fits the description mentioned in Daniel. This explains the all-out effort by the New Age, which is saturating our society with meditation right now. When this man comes forward, all those who are in touch with their higher self, those who are *enlightened*, will clearly recognize him as their unifier and give him their allegiance. He will have a ready-made constituency (many in key positions) to help him reconstruct society. This will be the final culmination of the paradigm shift.

A disciple of the Indian guru Rajneesh made this keen observation, illustrating the potential power of this deception and the hypnotic influence of the Coming One:

> Something had happened to Rajneesh that made him unlike other men. He had undergone some change—enlightenment, the rising of kundalini [serpent power]—and his being had been altered in palpable [noticeable] ways. The change in him in turn affected his sannyasins [disciples] and created a persistent and catalyzing resonance between them.[6]

What was the nature of the resonance? The Bible predicts the Antichrist shall worship a god of forces, and he and the false prophet will perform lying wonders (Revelation 13). Alice Bailey described the work of her New Age Christ very explicitly:

> The work of the Christ (two thousand years ago)
> was to proclaim certain great possibilities and the
> existence of great powers. His work when He reap-
> pears will be to prove the fact of these possibilities
> and to reveal the true nature and potency of man.[7]

The following is another powerful example of what this could
mean. A Hindu spiritual teacher named Sri Chinmoy demonstrated an
ability to lift 7000 pounds with one arm. Twenty spectators witnessed
this and recorded it by photograph and video. He attributed his impressive ability to *meditation power* and admits that without it he could
not lift 60 pounds.[8] What had most likely enabled him to do this was
the power of familiar spirits giving him (and those observing this) the
impression this was done through the power of his higher self. This is
what the Bible means by *lying wonders*. The Man of Sin (the Coming
One) will do this on a vast scale. He will seem to work great miracles
to convince humanity we all have this great power, or as Bailey called
it, potency within us.

An American woman with a secular worldview took a trip to
Brazil to study a Brazilian New Age *healer*. The impact he had on
her was quite remarkable. She recounted:

> Instantly my body felt as though it were filled with
> white light and I became weak in my knees and I started
> swaying. Soon, I became unable to stand, and some-
> one helped me to sit in a chair. Thereafter, I felt
> extreme heat beating down into my head, particularly
> on the left side. All during this experience, I was com-
> pletely conscious and my body was filled with waves
> of ecstasy. I had heard about and visualized white light
> before, but had never experienced being totally infused
> with it. I immediately made an association to the heal-
> ing power of Jesus Christ, and had no doubts that this

was the nature of the energy being transmitted to me.[9]

If this individual could do something of this nature on one woman, could not someone who really had the power of occultism behind him do the same thing on a large scale? He would in essence *Reiki* the whole world.

Mystery Babylon

Familiar spirits (fallen angels) will not just mislead a few individuals; they will deceive the whole world toward a new system. Satan (which means adversary) will be the power behind the *Coming One*—the great Antichrist. The origin of the Antichrist's religious system is clearly revealed by the apostle John in Revelation 17:5: "And on her forehead a name was written: Mystery, Babylon the Great, the mother of harlots and of the abominations of the earth."

Another word for Babylon in the Old Testament was Chaldea. The Chaldeans were renowned for their use of the metaphysical arts. They began the first mystery schools. Daniel 4:7 says: "Then the magicians, the astrologers, the Chaldeans, and the soothsayers came in." This Mystery Babylon, then, would be the original source or mother of what is now New Age metaphysics.

Thus, when the apostle John identifies the Antichrist's spiritual format, he is making reference to the city and the people that first spawned occultism in ancient times. All of the other mystery schools flowed out of Babylon, teaching essentially the same thing—the higher self. John saw it as one unbroken line throughout history culminating in the Antichrist's rule with hundreds of millions being given over to familiar spirits. Luke, who wrote the book of Acts, gave us an account of this activity as the first century believers were daily confronting spirits not of God:

> But there was a certain man called Simon, who previously practiced sorcery in the city and astonished

> the people of Samaria, claiming that he was some-
> one great, to whom they all gave heed, from the
> least to the greatest, saying, "This man is the great
> power of God." And they heeded him because he
> had astonished them with his sorceries for a long
> time. (Acts 8:9-11)

Simon was a man whose activities appeared good; otherwise the people would not have felt "this man is the great power of God." But the truth of the matter is, he wasn't of God—he just appeared to be. Fortunately for Simon, he repented from his Chaldean practice, and he and his household were saved.

Simon's conversion (like all conversions) is a huge threat to the mystical agenda. Hence, it is easy to see why the coming of the Christian gospel to the town of Ephesus was a great hindrance to the practice of occultism. Once the people understood they had been deceived by what appeared to be spiritual truth, they repented and liberated themselves of all their collections of mystical reci-pes. The following is a dramatic event:

> And many who had believed came confessing and
> telling their deeds. Also, many of those who had
> practiced magic brought their books together and
> burned them in the sight of all. And they counted
> up the value of them, and it totaled fifty thousand
> pieces of silver. So the word of the Lord grew might-
> ily and prevailed. (Acts 19:18-20)

The magical or metaphysical arts went out the door when the Gospel of Christ came in. The two were not only incompatible but totally opposite. Further, what the new believers burned equaled the wages of 150 men for one year. The Ephesian believers gave up their wealth and mystical formulas for the truth found in Jesus Christ. Unfortunately, the opposite is happening in the world today!

There is another account in Scripture that highlights what I want to reveal. It is found in Acts 16:16-19:

> Now it happened, as we went to prayer, that a cer-
> tain slave girl possessed with a spirit of divination
> met us, who brought her masters much profit by
> fortune-telling. This girl followed Paul and us, and
> cried out, saying, "These men are the servants of
> the Most High God, who proclaim to us the way of
> salvation." And this she did for many days. But Paul,
> greatly annoyed, turned and said to the spirit, "I
> command you in the name of Jesus Christ to come
> out of her!" And he came out that very hour. But
> when her masters saw that their hope of profit was
> gone, they seized Paul and Silas and dragged them
> into the marketplace to the authorities.

Such events in Scripture illustrate several things critical to understanding the nature and aim of familiar spirits:

- The spirit was the source of her power, not some
  latent faculty inherent in the human makeup. When it
  left, her ability was gone.

- The spirit was accurate to a high degree. Otherwise she would
  not have brought her masters "much gain." You do not
  become a success with inconsistency.

- Paul and the spirit were *not on the same side*—all was not *one* here. This
  is quite evident by the fact he cast it out of her. Most important of all, the spirit tried to identify itself with God. It was
  crafty when it followed Paul and Silas, for it was saying the
  truth: "These men show us the way of salvation." This reveals that *Mystery Babylon* and its spirit guides will try to appear as being on God's side. Today, much of this occurrence is already happening in the name of Christianity.

Coming In His Name

I believe the Bible contains an important signal that the changes of times and seasons may indeed be at hand. In Matthew 24:3-5, which is a chapter dealing with the tribulation period, Jesus spoke these revealing words to His disciples concerning the signs of His coming and the end of the world (age):

> Now as He sat on the Mount of Olives, the disciples came to Him privately, saying, "Tell us when will these things be? And what will be the sign of Your coming, and of the end of the age?"
>
> And Jesus answered and said to them: "Take heed that no one deceives you. For *many will come in my name,* saying, "I am the Christ," and will deceive many. (emphasis mine)

I have heard two interpretations of Jesus' reply. The first interpretation asserts various individuals will claim to be the returned Jesus Christ. The other view says a number of messiah figures will appear and gather followers to themselves in a similar fashion to cultic leader Jim Jones or Bhagwan Shree Rajneesh, the guru leader who set up his utopia in Oregon. I now believe both of these interpretations do not encompass the bigger picture. It is in light of numerous New Age statements that Matthew 24 takes on new significance.

A basic tenet of New Age thinking is that of the *Master Jesus.* Adherents to this idea believe during the unrecorded period of His life, Jesus traveled to various occult centers and mystery schools in such places as Tibet, India, Persia, and Egypt; at these places Jesus learned the metaphysical secrets of the ages. Therefore, they claim Jesus spent seventeen years of travel on a pilgrimage of higher consciousness. According to this viewpoint, Jesus of Nazareth became the Master Jesus, one who has gained mastery over the physical world by becoming one with his higher self.

This is how the New Age interprets the word *Christ.* The word comes from the Greek word *kristos*, which means the anointed. New Agers believe this means being anointed or in touch with the higher self or divine nature. In other words, to be anointed is to be enlightened.

Since New Agers believe Jesus was completely in tune with his higher self, this made him a *Christ*. It is, they believe, a state of awareness and spiritual condition rather than a title. For that reason, anyone who is in full attunement with his or her *divine essence* is also a *Christ*.

After reading innumerable such statements that promoted this *Christ Consciousness*, I took a closer look at Matthew 24:5. What I found astounded me! The Greek word for *many* in this verse is *polus*, which means a very great or sore number. The word may actually be saying that millions upon millions of people are going to claim deity for themselves. The Greek words for "come in my name" means they shall come claiming to represent what He represents by using His name.

In summary, Matthew 24:5 is saying a great number of people shall come claiming to represent what He (Jesus) represents but will be in fact deceiving people. In light of the warning of Jesus ("many shall come in my name"), consider the following remarks taken from two New Age sources:

> Jesus was one soul who reached the state of Christ Consciousness; there have been many others. He symbolized the blueprint we must follow ... The way is open to everyone to become a Christ by achieving the Christ Consciousness through walking the same path He walked. He simply and beautifully demonstrated the pattern.[10]

> The significance of incarnation and resurrection is not that Jesus was a human like us but rather that *we are gods like him*—or at least have the potential to be. The significance of Jesus is not as a

vehicle of salvation but as a model of perfection. (emphasis mine)[11]

New Ager's claim Jesus is a model of what the New Age or
Aquarian person is to become. These statements could be called:
coming in His name or claiming to represent what He represents.

The remainder of verse five in Matthew, chapter 24, reveals
the warning of Jesus that they will actually say: "...I am Christ."
Again, we find a multitude of statements by New Agers that con-
firm the admonition of Jesus: Here are some examples:

> This World Leader, by the way, is supposed to represent the
> new Aquarian Age and establish the Oneness of all mankind—
> one religion ... In the Aquarian Age, you will not need the
> outer saviour, for you will be able to learn how to reach the
> inner Christ Consciousness ... The Saviour of the New Age
> will be a channel through which all Cosmic Truth will come.[12]

> The Christ is You. You are the one who is to come—each of
> you. Each and everyone of you![13]

> Christhood is not something to come at a point in the future
> when you are more evolved. Christhood is—right now! I am
> the Christ of God. *You are the Christ of God* (emphasis mine).[14]

It is not surprising to find those in the contemplative prayer
camp who also subscribe to this view. Contemplative author John
R. Yungblut, former Dean of Studies at the Quaker Meditation Center at Pendle Hill in Pennsylvania, echoed a similar notion:

> But we cannot confine the existence of the divine
> to this one man [Jesus] among men. Therefore we
> are not to worship the man Jesus, though we can-
> not refrain from worshiping the source of this Holy

Spirit or Christ-life, which for many of us has been
revealed primarily in this historical figure.[15]

Willigis Jager, who ironically, titled his book, *Contemplation: A Christian Path,* stated the same perception of Christ's role to humanity:

> Salvation will now be nothing other than a realization
> of the fact that "the kingdom of God is within you"
> … This is the Good News Jesus proclaimed to human-
> ity. The kingdom is *already within all of us* (emphasis
> mine).[16]

Although many contemplative authors such as Richard Foster
still maintain a traditional view of Christology, enough subscribe to
the New Age model that there is cause for grave concern.

There is also a movement occurring in Jewish circles that par-
allels the contemplative spirituality of Catholics and Protestants.
Based on the Kabbalah, the Jewish mystical text, this version of
contemplative prayer is spreading like wildfire through Judaism.
Take a look at any section on Judaism at a local bookstore and find
it saturated with books on this subject.

This new spirituality within Judaism is widely known as the *Jewish
Renewal* movement. This is significant to the prophecies of Matthew, chapter 24, because the mystic Jews also refer to the higher states they enter as
the "Messianic Consciousness."[17] So, in effect, to be in this state of being,
in their view, makes one a messiah or in the Greek language a christos—
a christ.

The Great Apostasy

In light of the many who will be coming in Christ's name, I also
believe the Alice Bailey prophecies can provide further insight into
what the apostle Paul called in II Thessalonians the *falling away.*
Bailey eagerly foretold of what she termed "the regeneration of
the churches."[18] Her rationale for this was obvious:

> The Christian church in its many branches can serve
> as a St. John the Baptist, as a voice crying in the
> wilderness, and as a nucleus through which world
> illumination may be accomplished.[19]

In other words, instead of opposing Christianity, the occult would capture Christianity and then use it as a vehicle for spreading New Age consciousness! The various churches would still have their outer forms of Christianity and still use much of the same lingo. If asked certain questions about traditional Christian doctrine, the same answers would be given. But it would all be on the outside; on the inside a contemplative spirituality would be drawing in those open to it.

In wide segments of Christendom this has indeed already occurred. As stated earlier, Thomas Keating alone taught 31,000 people mystical prayer in one year. People are responding to this in large numbers because it has the external appearance of Christianity but in truth, is the total opposite—a skillful spiritual delusion. I believe what we are seeing here is the *falling away* Paul speaks of:

> Let no one deceive you by any means: for that Day
> will not come unless the falling away comes first,
> and the man of sin is revealed, the son of perdition
> (II Thessalonians 2:3).

Note this departure is tied in with the revelation of the Man of Sin. If he is indeed Bailey's Coming One, then both prophecies, Bailey's and Paul's, fit together perfectly—but obviously, from opposite perspectives.

This is very logical when one sees, as Paul proclaimed, that they will fall away to "the mystery of iniquity" (II Thessalonians 2:7). The word here in Greek is the same word we derive mysticism from. The departure is to occult mysticism!

The most logical reason for this revitalization of Christendom is that it must be able to fit in with Bailey's "new and vital world religion"[20]—a religion that would be the cornerstone of the New

Age. Such a religion would be the spiritual platform for the Coming One. This unity of spiritual thought would not be a single one-world denomination but would have a unity-in-diversity agenda. Thomas Merton made a direct reference to this at a spiritual summit conference in Calcutta, India when he told Hindus and Buddhists: "We are already one but we imagine we are not. What we have to recover is our original unity."[21]

One can easily find numerous such appeals like Merton's in contemplative writings. Examine the following:

> The Christian is not to become a Hindu or a Buddhist, nor a Hindu or a Buddhist to become a Christian. But each must assimilate the spirit of the others ... —Vivakananda[22]

> It is my sense, from having meditated with persons from many different [non-Christian] traditions, that in the silence we experience *a deep unity*. When we go beyond the portals of the rational mind into the experience, there is only *one God to be experienced.* (emphasis mine) —Basil Pennington[23]

> The new ecumenism involved here is not between Christian and Christian, but between Christians and the grace of other intuitively deep religious traditions. —Tilden Edwards[24]

I observed this "new ecumenism" in a syndicated article featured in one regional Catholic newspaper. The article proclaimed that the "word of God" can also be found in Eastern religions. A Catholic retreat master offered the notion that "today Catholics have an obligation to seek God in other traditions."[25]

This view is not just an isolated fluke. This is what I refer to as mertonization (remaining in the religion you already are in but being aligned with Eastern mysticism). This is Merton's dream fulfilled: mystical unity within religious diversity. In effect that one-world religion is here now!

Satan's plan has always been to deceive people into believing they can become like God. God has given Satan the freedom to carry out his plans, and he has certain powers to recruit humans in attempting to complete it. Consequently, it is not inconceivable that Satan is revealing these things to whom he wants. I believe Alice Bailey was one of those he chose to lay out this program. Therefore, Bailey's predictions can indeed be factual and not just the fanciful meandering of a fertile imagination. When the depth and intricate detail of her work is studied, it cannot be dismissed as trivial. One author made the following keen observation on this point: "Alice Bailey's gigantic corpus of wisdom could not have been invented by human minds; the teachings are undoubtedly superhuman in origin."[26]

I consider Alice Bailey as an apostle of occultism, and her writings as mystical revelations. She is telling the world the path it will be taking and how it is going to be done—in essence, a combined manifesto and blueprint. The fact that much of what she predicted has indeed actually happened gives even greater credence that her work really is the design for the one Paul called "the son of perdition."

"Rethinking" the Gospel

Various church statements reflect Bailey's dark prophecies that speak to the "revitalization" of the churches. Even now a recent Catholic dictionary states: "Current ideas about mysticism underscore that it is for the many, not just a chosen few."[27] A recent article in *America*, a national Catholic magazine, shows the result of this mysticism in regard to evangelization. The article entitled, *Rethinking Missions in India*, states the *spirit* is active in Hinduism as much as Christianity and therefore both religions "are co-pilgrims on the way to fulfillment."[28] The significance of this is clearly revealed in the following view from the same article:

> Any claims to superiority are damaging. Religions need not be compared. All we are expected to do is to serve man by revealing to him the love of God made manifest in Jesus Christ.[29]

What is happening here is a complete turnaround in the real meaning of evangelization. In truth, if you want to reveal to man the love of God, manifest in Jesus Christ, you proclaim the *blood of Christ* for salvation! It is vital to note the article says this new approach is " ... indissolubly linked to contemplation."[30]

The April 28th, 2002 edition of the PBS series Religion and Ethics Weekly also revealed the findings of a national poll conducted by them and U.S. News & World Report magazine. The findings spoke for themselves. According to their poll, 77 percent of all Americans feel all religions have elements of the truth, not just one religion alone. The polls also said 70 percent of *Christians* say other religions should *not* be the targets of conversion efforts. The unconverted should be left alone. Only 24 percent of *Christians* thought an attempt should be made to convert members of other religions to Christianity.

This means that, if this poll is accurate, only one out of every four Christians in the country believes that Christianity has the corner on presenting the way to heaven and salvation.

There *are* things that are true in other religions such as morals and ethics, but if they lack the core message of Christianity can they really be true?

The view that *all* religions have "elements" of the truth fits the Merton/Nouwen notion of salvation more than the one the apostles of the New Testament held. What the other religions lack is a *Savior* and in Christianity His name is the Lord Jesus Christ.

The point here should be obvious. If 70 percent of all Christians believe that those in other religions should not be actively reached for Jesus Christ then they are, in effect, saying Jesus is *my* way but your way (e.g. the higher self, the Buddha, nature) is equally fine.

Its not that much of a step further to start to see Jesus as a model rather than a Savior, one of many manifestations of God rather than the *only* manifestation of God.

For those who are skeptical of a world-mysticism that could become pervasive, I suggest they carefully reflect on the words of popular seminar leader, John Gray, a T.M. practitioner and author of the

best-seller, *Men Are From Mars, Women Are From Venus*. He has revealed
how easily and quickly people are moving into the mystical realm:

> I lived as a monk in the mountains of Switzerland
> for nine years to experience my inner connection to
> God. Now, when I teach meditation, I see people
> progressing light-years faster than I did. Within a
> few weeks, they begin to experience the current of
> energy flowing in their fingertips. Ninety percent
> of the people who learn to meditate at my seminars
> have this experience in one or two days. To me, this
> is extremely exciting.
>
> Throughout history this has never happened. To have
> such an immediate experience was unheard of. The
> great mystics and saints of our past had to spend years
> waiting to have a spiritual experience, and now practi-
> cally anyone can experience the current of energy.[31]

I believe the Holy Spirit is starting to take off the brakes. The
holding back effect Paul spoke of in II Thessalonians 2:6 is beginning
to recede. The Lord is going to allow the man of lawlessness to emerge
at the proper time. Now is the time for each person to decide where
he or she is going to stand. There may not be a lot of time left.

The world is opening its arms to a new spirituality that will allow
diversity to exist under the umbrella of mysticism. The correlating
theme will be—we are all One. Further, not only will the man of
lawlessness rise to power with a one-world economy and political
base but with him will come a contemplative spirituality that will
allow many to find their own *Christ Consciousness*.

7

Seducing Spirits

I once heard a radio interview with Richard Foster that revealed the high regard in which many evangelicals of influence hold him. The talk show host made his own admiration obvious with such comments to Foster as, "You have heard from God ... this is a message of enormous value," and in saying Foster's work was a "curriculum for Christ-likeness." I found this praise especially disturbing after Foster stated in the interview that Christianity was "not complete without the contemplative dimension."[1] Of course, my concern was that Foster's *curriculum* would result in Thomas Merton-likeness instead.

When I look ahead and ponder the impact of this book, unquestionably, there are some very sobering considerations. The contemplative prayer movement has already planted strong roots within evangelical Christianity. Many sincere, devout and respected Christians have embraced Thomas Merton's vision that:

> The most important need in the Christian world today is this inner truth nourished by this Spirit of contemplation ... Without contemplation and interior prayer the Church cannot fulfill her mission to transform and save mankind.[2]

A statement like this should immediately alert the discerning Christian that something is wrong. It is the gospel that saves mankind, not the silence. When Merton says "save," he really means *enlighten.* Remember, Merton's spiritual worldview was panentheistic oneness.

Some will see this book as divisive and intolerant—especially those who share Merton's view of the future. Pastors may be set at odds with one another and possibly with their congregations, friends, and even family members who may be divided on the issues of contemplative spirituality. Nevertheless, having weighed the pros and cons of writing this book, I am prepared to receive the inevitable responses from fans of these contemplative mentors. And although I sincerely feel goodwill toward those I have critiqued, I am convinced the issues covered in this book are of such vital importance I am willing to bear the burden.

After taking an honest look at the evidence, the conclusion is overwhelming that contemplative prayer is not a justifiable practice for Christians. The errors of contemplative spirituality are simple and clear for the following three reasons:

- It is not found in the Bible.
- It correlates with occult methods (i.e., mantra, vain repetition).
- It is sympathetic with Eastern mystical perceptions (God in everything; all is One–Panentheism).

These are well-documented facts, not just opinions. Furthermore, the contemplative prayer movement is uniform, indicating a link to a central source of knowledge. Based on the above facts, we know what that source is.

The apostle Paul warns us of seducing spirits in his first letter to Timothy: "Now the Spirit expressly says that in latter times some will depart from the faith, giving heed to deceiving [seducing] spirits and doctrines of demons" (I Tim. 4:1).

The operative word here is "deceiving" or *seducing* which means to be an *impostor* or to *mislead.* It is plain to see a real delusion is going on—or as Paul called it, a seduction. How then can you tell if you are a victim yourself? It is actually not that difficult.

The doctrines (instructions) of demons (no matter how nice, how charming, how devoted to God they sound) convey that everything has Divine Presence (all is One). This is clear heresy—for that would be saying Satan and God are one also. If what Henri Nouwen proclaimed is true when he said, "We can come to the full realization of the unity of all that is," then Jesus Christ and Satan are also united. That, my friend, is something only a demonic spirit would teach!

An even more subtle yet seductive idea says: Without a mystical technique, God is somehow indifferent or unapproachable. Those of you who are parents can plainly see the falsehood of this. Do your children need a method to capture your full attention or guidance? Of course not! If you love your children, you will care for and interact with them because you want to participate with them. The same is true of God's attention towards those He has called his own.

The central role of a shepherd is to guide and direct the sheep. The sheep know the voice of their Master by simply following Him in faith (John 10:14-18). The Shepherd does not expect or desire the sheep to perform a method or religious technique to be close to Him. He has already claimed them as His own. Remember! Religiosity is *man's* way to God while Christianity is *God's* way to man. Contemplative prayer is just another man-inspired attempt to get to God.

When we receive Christ, we receive the Holy Spirit—thus we receive God. Christians do not have to search for some esoteric technique to draw closer to God. The fullness of God has already taken residency in those who have received Christ. The Christian's response is not to search for God through a method but simply to yield his or her will to the will of God.

When looking at principles like these, Paul's warning becomes clear. A seduction will not work if the seducee is wise to the ways of the seducer.

Christians must not be led purely by their emotions; there must be ground rules. A popular saying is: "You can't put God in a box."

That is correct in some ways, but it's not true if the box is the Bible. God will not work outside of what He has laid down in His message to humanity.

The answer to the contemplative prayer movement is simple. A Christian is complete in Christ. The argument that contemplative prayer can bring a fuller measure of God's love, guidance, direction and nurturing is the epitome of dishonor to Jesus Christ, the Good Shepherd. It is, in essence, anti-Christian.

The late Dr. Paul Bubna, President of the Christian and Missionary Alliance wrote in an article, *Purveyors of Grace or Ungrace*:

> Knowing Christ is a journey of solid theological understanding. It is the Holy Spirit's illuminating the Scriptures to our darkened minds and hearts that give birth to the wonder of unconditional love.[3]

The contemplative message has deeply maligned this wonderful work of God's grace and the sanctifying work of the Holy Spirit. The Holy Spirit is the one who guides the Christian into all truth. Those who have the Holy Spirit indwelling them do not need the silence. The Christian hears the voice of Jehovah through the Holy Spirit, not through contemplative prayer. Jesus made it clear He is the one who initiates this process, not man:

> If you love me, keep my commandments. And I will pray the Father, and He will give you another Helper, that He may abide with you forever—the Spirit of truth, whom the world cannot receive, because it neither sees Him nor knows Him; but you know Him, for He dwells with you and will be in you. (John 14:15-17)

This is Not From Me!

Pastor Ron Comer, my good friend who wrote the foreword for this book, first became aware of the dangers of contemplative prayer when he was seeking the guidance of the Holy Spirit. As the youth pastor of a large, dynamic evangelical church, he longed to draw closer to God and hear His voice. He shared with me the following story of how he heard the voice of the Lord, but it was a much different outcome than what he expected. He spoke of how God's grace rescued him from seducing spirits. I'll let him recount his own experience with contemplative prayer:

> One day I decided to lock myself in my office and not come out until I knew I had met God. I took from my shelf a book by Richard Foster called *Celebration of Discipline*. I had briefly read it years before but did not give much attention to its practical application. Now, as I began to read, I was intrigued by the freshness of Foster's approach. It seemed so freeing to come before God and just empty me of myself. I knew God could not fill me if self was in the way.
>
> I laid the book on the floor and got on my knees. I began to step through Foster's teachings of how to come before God. I emptied my mind of all thought and began to repeat sacred words that brought praise to God. I found myself repeating the same words over and over. After a period of about two hours, I began to feel a release from all my cares. As contrary as it seems, my body began to feel an energy that was both exciting and relaxing. My mind was at peace and my spirit open to any experience God would share with me. I began to slip into a euphoric, mystical state. Suddenly, I was struck by five powerful words that penetrated every sense of my existence. The words were firm but loving. My inner

spirit had never heard such clarity. The five words were, "This is not from Me!"

> Immediately upon hearing these words I began to grieve at all I was doing, and I repented—feeling polluted and foolish. I quickly realized I had not been enjoying God but had opened my mind and heart to a seducing spirit. God ended this episode by confirming in my spirit I needed to stay alert and discerning for deceptive spirits that were amazingly good at emulating the Spirit of God and masquerading as angels of light.

I realize Pastor Ron's experience is highly subjective. After all, what if it was God he was really getting and a familiar spirit who intervened, derailing a genuine godly encounter? I also understand how insulting this account might be to Foster himself and to those evangelicals who admire him and consider his work valuable. It belittles their power of discernment and implies a lack of theological sophistication. In addition, who would want to hurt a man's ministry simply because a youth pastor heard a voice. Nevertheless, the voice of warning Ron heard lines up with and reflects a warning from Scripture: " … test the spirits" (I John 4:1).

Let's test them using Foster's teaching once again. In his book, *Celebration of Discipline,* he devotes a number of pages to what he calls the *Biblical basis* for this sort of prayer. He makes reference to many instances throughout the Bible where God talked to people, such as Christ teaching people after His resurrection—in other words, encounters between man and Divinity. But Foster then jumps straight to contemplative prayer, leading the reader to think this is how it is done when, in fact, he has not really presented a Biblical basis for using the repetition of sacred words at all. He goes right to the contemplative mystics to legitimize his teachings when he writes:

How sad that contemporary Christians are so ignorant of the vast sea of literature on Christian meditation by faithful believers throughout the centuries! And their testimony to the joyful life of perpetual communion is amazingly uniform.[4]

That is the problem. The contemplative authors *are* "amazingly uniform." Even though they all profess a love for God and Jesus, they have each added something, which is contrary to what God conveys in His written word.

Contemplative mystic John R. Yungblut penned the following observation that rings true for almost all such contemplative practitioners. He concludes, "The core of the mystical experience is the apprehension of unity, and the perception of relatedness. For the mystics the world is one."[5]

Panentheism is the bedrock of the contemplative prayer movement; therefore the establishment of whether or not it is Biblically valid is imperative.

Foster also believes, as discussed earlier in this chapter, that God's ability to impact the non-contemplative Christian is limited. Foster expresses, "What happens in meditation is that we create the emotional and spiritual space which allows Christ to construct an inner sanctuary in the heart."[6]

But as I stated, the Trinity already has an inner sanctuary in every Christian. It is being in Christ (via the Holy Spirit) that allows every believer to receive guidance and direction.

Furthermore, when Richard Foster cites those like Sue Monk Kidd as examples of what he is promoting (as he does in his book, *Prayer: Finding the Heart's True Home),* it is reasonable then to expect that if you engage in Foster's prayer methods, you will become like his examples.

Monk Kidd's spirituality is spelled out clearly in her book, *When The Heart Waits.* She explains:

> There's a bulb of truth buried in the human soul
> [not just Christian] that's only God … the soul is
> more than something to win or save. It's the seat
> and repository of the inner Divine, the God-image,
> the truest part of us.[7]

Sue Monk Kidd, an introspective woman, gives a revealing description of her spiritual transformation in her book, *God's Joyful Surprise: Finding Yourself Loved.* She shares how she suffered a deep hollowness and spiritual hunger for many years even though she was very active in her Baptist church.[8] She sums up her feelings:

> Maybe we sense we're disconnected from God
> somehow. He becomes superfluous to the business
> at hand. He lives on the periphery so long we begin
> to think that is where He belongs. Anything else
> seems unsophisticated or fanatical.[9]

Ironically, a Sunday school co-worker handed her a book by Thomas Merton telling her she needed to read it. Once Monk Kidd read it, her life changed dramatically.

What happened next completely reoriented Sue Monk Kidd's worldview and belief system. She started down the contemplative prayer road with bliss, reading numerous books and repeating the sacred word methods taught in her readings.[10] She ultimately came to the mystical realization that:

> I am speaking of recognizing the hidden truth that
> we are one with all people. We are part of them and
> they are part of us … When we encounter another
> person, … we should walk as if we were upon holy
> ground. We should respond as if God dwells there.[11]

One could come to Monk Kidd's defense by saying she is just referring to Christians and non-Christians sharing a common humanity and the need to treat people well. While respecting humanity is important, she fails to distinguish between Christians and non-Christians thereby negating Christ's imperative, "You must be born again" (John 3:7), as the prerequisite for the indwelling of God. Her mystical universalism is apparent when she quotes someone who advises that the Hindu greeting namaste, which translates, *I honor the God in you*, should be used by Christians.[12]

Monk Kidd, like Merton, did not join a metaphysical church such as the Unity Church or a Religious Science church. She found her spirituality within the comfortable and familiar confines of a Baptist church!

Moreover, when Sue Monk Kidd found her universal spirituality she was no teenager. She was a sophisticated, mature family woman. This illustrates the susceptibility of the millions like her who are seeking seemingly novel, positive approaches to Christian spiritual growth. Those who lack discernment are at great risk. What looks godly or spiritually benign on the surface may have principles behind it that are really at odds with Christianity.

If Foster uses these kinds of mystics as contemplative prayer models without disclaimers regarding their universalist beliefs (like Sue Monk Kidd), then it is legitimate to question whether or not he also is sympathetic to the same beliefs as theirs. At the Foster seminar I attended, a colleague of his assured the audience that when they were in this state, they could just "smell the gospel." Based on the research of this movement, what you can smell is not the gospel but the Ganges![13]

Merton or the Holy Spirit

Two authors from Great Britain portrayed a stunningly clear picture of New Age spirituality. They explained:

> [T]he keynote of it appears to be a movement for synthesis derived from an understanding of the underlying unity behind all things and the sense of

oneness that this brings ... This oneness of all life is
the crux of the New Age movement.[14]

M. Basil Pennington defined the contemplative spiritual worldview
in his book, *Thomas Merton My Brother*. He related:

> The Spirit enlightened him [Merton] in the true syn-
> thesis [unity] of all and in the harmony of that huge
> chorus of living beings. In the midst of it he lived
> out a vision of a new world, where all divisions have
> fallen away and the divine goodness is perceived and
> enjoyed as present in all and through all.[15]

The first viewpoint describes God as the oneness of all exist-
ence. In Merton's new world, God is perceived as being present
"in all and through all." It is clear the same spirit enlightened both
parties. The only difference was Merton's revelation worked in a
Christian context just as Alice Bailey predicted. Unfortunately, this
context is now commonplace in Catholic circles, becoming so in
mainline Protestant churches, and being eagerly explored by an
ever-increasing number of evangelical Christians.

Evangelical leaders must now debate whether or not such
spiritual truths as resting in God are the same as contemplative
silence. Based on these presented documentations I believe contemplative prayer practice has no place in true Christianity. Scripture clearly teaches that with salvation comes an automatic guidance system—the Holy Spirit. Lewis Sperry Chafer in his out-
standing book, *Grace The Glorious Theme*, spelled out this truth
with crystal clarity:

> It is stated in Romans 5:5 that "the Holy Spirit who
> was given to us." This is true of every person who
> is saved. The Spirit is the birthright in the new life.
> By Him alone can the character and service that
> belongs to the normal daily life of the Christian be

realized. The Spirit is the "All-Sufficient One." Every victory in the new life is gained by His strength, and every reward in glory will be won only as a result of His enabling power.[16]

I put forth this challenge to all who read this book. Show me a Scripture in the New Testament in which the Holy Spirit is activated or accessed by contemplative prayer. If such a verse exists, wouldn't it be the keynote verse in defense of contemplative prayer?

None exists!

I want to emphasize in this chapter what I believe cuts through all the emotional appeal that has attracted so many to teachers like Foster and Manning and really boils the issue down to its clearest state.

In Richard Foster's most recent book, *Streams of Living Water*, Foster emanates his hoped–for vision of an "all inclusive community" that he feels God is forming today. He sees this as "a great new gathering of the people of God."[17]

On the surface this might sound noble and sanctifying, but a deeper examination will expose elements that line up more with Alice Bailey's vision than with Jesus Christ's.

Foster prophesies: "I see a Catholic monk from the hills of Kentucky standing alongside a Baptist evangelist from the streets of Los Angeles and together offering up a sacrifice of praise. I see a people."[18]

The only place in "the hills of Kentucky" where Catholic monks live is the Gethsemane Abbey, a Trappist monastery. This also, coincidentally, was the home base of Thomas Merton.

Let me explain this significant connection. In the summer of 1996, Buddhist and Catholic monks met together to dialogue in what was billed the "Gethsemane Encounter."[19] David Steidl-Rast, a zen-Buddhist trained monk and close friend of Thomas Merton, facilitated this event.

During the encounter, presentations on zen meditation and practice from the Theravedan Buddhist tradition were offered.[20] One of the speakers discussed the "correlation of the Christian contemplative life with the lives of our Buddhist sisters and brothers."[21]

For these monks and the Baptist evangelist to be "a people," as Richard Foster says, someone has to change. Either the monks have to abandon their Buddhist convictions and align with the Baptists, or the Baptists have to become contemplative style Baptists and embrace the monks' beliefs. That is the dilemma in Foster's "great gathering of God."

David Steidl-Rast once asked Thomas Merton what role Buddhism played in his going deeper into the spiritual life. Merton replied quite frankly: "I think I couldn't understand Christian teaching the way I do if it were not in the light of Buddhism."[22]

Did Merton mean that in order to understand what Christianity really is, you have to change your consciousness? I believe that is exactly what he meant. Once he personally did that through contemplative prayer, Buddhism provided him with the explanation of what he experienced. But the catalyst was changing his consciousness. This is what I am warning Christians about. Contemplative prayer is presenting a way to God identical with all the world's mystical traditions. Christians are lulled into it by the emphasis on seeking the Kingdom of God and greater piety, yet the apostle Paul put the church's end-times apostasy in the context of a *mystical* seduction. If this practice doesn't fit that description, I don't know what does. You don't have to change your consciousness to grab "aholt" of God. All you must do is become born-again. What Steidl-Rast and the other Gethsemane monks should have been telling Buddhists is, "Behold! The Lamb of God, who takes away the sin of the world!" (John 1:29).

In his book, *Ruthless Trust*, Brennan Manning mentions that Sue Monk Kidd eventually came under the mentorship of Dr. Beatrice Bruteau who authored the book, *What We Can Learn From The East*. Since that title is self explanatory one can understand why Dr. Bruteau would write the preface to a book like *The Mystic Heart* by Brother Wayne Teasdale. In the preface she touts that a universal spirituality based on mysticism is going to save the world.

It is obvious that all of these people want a better world. They are not sinister conspirators like those out of a James Bond film. It is their *niceness* that rejects the reality of the fundamental separation between Man and God. It is their sense of compassion that feeds their universalism. It is idealism that makes Manning so attractive and causes him to say that Dr. Bruteau is a "trustworthy guide to contemplative consciousness."[23]

The Christian of the Future?

The cover of the July/August 1999 issue of *Group Magazine*, a leading resource magazine for Christian youth leaders, featured a teenage girl, eyes shut, doing contemplative prayer. The article, "Ancient-Future Youth Ministry" begins by declaring:

> It's Sunday just after 5 P.M.. in the youth room … Seven adults are sitting around a "Christ-candle" in the youth room. There is no talking, no laughter. For 10 minutes, the only noise is the sound of their breathing … now it's 7 p.m. — one hour into the night's youth group gathering. There are 18 senior highers and five adults sitting in a candlelit sanctuary. A gold cross stands on a table … They're chanting the "Jesus Prayer," an ancient meditative practice.[24]

According to this article two Christian organizations, Youth Specialties and San Francisco Theological Seminary (Presbyterian Church, USA), have teamed together to do a three-year test project to develop an approach to youth ministry that incorporates contemplative practices.[25] These two organizations are sponsoring the project in 16 churches of various denominations. The article was very open to the fact that sacred word repetition was at the heart of this project. The article revealed that, in all 16 test congregations, middle school and senior high youth "were eager to learn contemplative spiritual practices."[26] One of the church's associate pastors even went so far as to say, "We shouldn't be surprised it's working so well. It's kind of a no-brainer. If you make the space, the Spirit will come."[27] According to the project's mission statement this model will soon be "made immediately available to youth ministries nationwide."[28]

How widespread could this become? In the fall of 1997 the Lilly Endowment funded this ministry experiment called the Youth Ministry and Spirituality Project. The project directors are Mark Yaconelli (son of Mike Yaconelli) and Andrew Dreitcer. Mike Yaconelli is co-founder of Youth Specialties, a resource and training organization that has a major impact upon evangelical youth work across America. These men teach courses at the Youth Specialties National Youth Workers Conventions and the Canadian National Youth Workers Conventions. Course titles include, "Space for God: a Contemplative Model of Youth Ministry," and "God Encounters: Spiritual Exercises That Transform Students." In addition, Youth Specialties holds a national convention for pastors each year, three national youth worker conventions a year and over 100 seminars every year that reach over 100,000 youth workers worldwide—all with its current teaching on spirituality.

Mike Yaconelli's attraction and acceptance of contemplative prayer is very similar to the story of Sue Monk Kidd. In his book, *Dangerous Wonder*, Yaconelli relates how lost he had felt after twenty-five years of ministry. In his confusion he read Henri Nouwen's book, *In The Name of Jesus*, and found himself wanting "to start listening again to the voice of Jesus."[29]

In Nouwen's book we can find the method that began Yaconelli's claim to a newfound voice of Jesus:

> Through the discipline of contemplative prayer, Christian leaders have to learn to listen again and again to the voice of love and to find there the wisdom and courage to address whatever issue presents itself to them ... For Christian leadership to be truly fruitful in the future, a movement from the moral to the mystical is required.[30]

Yaconelli took this admonition to heart and is now not only practicing Nouwen's prayer method but is also promoting it through his powerful organization.

If this mystical paradigm shift were, indeed, accomplished, what would Christians of the future be like? If Christians developed into the spiritual likeness of Henri Nouwen you would find them meditating with Buddhists as Nouwen did—which he called "dialogue of the heart."[31] You would also find them listening to tapes on the *seven* chakras[32] (which Reiki is based on), which Nouwen did, and above all you would find them wanting to help people "claim his or her own way to God"[33] (universalism) (see chapter three), as Nouwen did. Nouwen wrote that his solitude, and the solitude of his Buddhist friends, would "greet each other and support each other."[34] In this one statement lies the fundamental flaw of the contemplative prayer movement—spiritual adultery.

Buddhism proclaims there is nothing outside of yourself needed for salvation. One Buddhist teacher wrote, "The Buddhist approach states that what is ultimately required for human fulfillment is a perfection of being that is found in who we already are."[35] A Christian is one who looks to Jesus Christ as his or her Savior, so to honor the Buddhist approach is to deny the One who gave Himself for us. It is logically impossible to claim Christianity and Buddhism as both being true because each promote a different basis for salvation. Jesus said, *"I am the door. If anyone enters by Me, he will be saved ... "* (John 10:9). You cannot love and follow the teachings of both Buddha and Jesus—for in reality the choice is either trusting in a self-deity or Jesus Christ as Lord and Savior.

The only way Nouwen's contemplative prayer could support the Buddhist view is if it shares the same mysticism, which is the point I am trying to prove in this book. I believe the facts speak for themselves. This is also the same mysticism many seek to embed in the heart of evangelical Christianity.

The question may arise—how can credible evangelical organizations justify meditative practices that clearly resemble those of Eastern meditation? As pointed out earlier in this book, Christian terminology surrounds these practices. It only takes a few credible Christian leaders with national profiles, to embrace a teaching that *sounds* Christian to affect large numbers in the church. Moreover, we have many trusting Christians who do not use the Scriptures to test the claims of others. Building an entire prayer method around an out-of-context verse or two is presumptuous at best. At this juncture of time, it is critical that Christians devote themselves to serious Bible study and discernment regarding this issue.

In the spiritual climate of today a unifying mystical prayer practice fits the paradigm necessary to unite the various world faiths. In Western civilization, this model is the contemplative prayer movement. I believe this movement is on the slippery slope that will lead to the great apostasy. For this to happen, as the Bible says, there will be "seducing spirits" who design a spirituality very closely related to the truth. Every Christian must therefore discern whether or not the contemplative prayer movement is a deeper way of walking with God or a deception that is attempting to undermine the very gospel itself.

When individuals such as Thomas Merton want to integrate the East's mystical insights into Christianity then there has occurred a fundamental betrayal of the Christian message. And when men like Nouwen, Foster and Manning become cheerleaders for the mystical prayer methods that caused Merton to follow this path, you have to question the validity of their writings on that subject.

Jesus Christ has called His church to be sanctified (set apart for holy purposes), Spirit-filled (consumed with His presence), surrendered (to Him alone), and willing to suffer (for the sake of righteousness). The world is going to offer many spiritual experiences while we quickly move toward a time where the masses will conform to a universal spirituality that proclaims the oneness of all things. This global spirituality could be the platform that ushers in the False Messiah. Knowing this, let us take the warnings about false teaching seriously and call upon God's grace and mercy for discerning hearts and minds.

Perhaps we might receive some indication of the pervasive

impact of this universal spirituality by taking a look at a most sobering reality. According to one Reiki center, in Germany alone in 1996 there were over one million Reiki students.[36] In a population of only 80 million, this number is astounding. If each of the students performs Reiki on just one person a month, in less than a year's time nearly 15% of Germany's population could be under the spiritual influence of Reiki. Potentially today, over 90% of the country's population may have come into contact with a Reiki practitioner at some time. Considering the spiritual aspects of Reiki this has significant implications for the whole world!

Simultaneously contemplative prayer also stands on the threshold of exploding worldwide. Dr. Larry Crabb, spiritual director for the 50,000 member American Association of Christian Counselors, has written the foreword to a recent book that expounds on the future of spiritual direction in the evangelical church. The authors the book promotes are the same ones that *A Time of Departing* focuses on: Nouwen, Merton, Foster, Keating, Pennington, etc. It is safe to assume then that we are looking at a contemplative approach. With that in mind, Dr. Crabb predicted: "The spiritual climate is ripe. Jesus seekers across the world are being prepared to abandon the old way of the written code for the new way of the Spirit."[37]

Let us be mindful that deception is subtle, and we must be alert. All of life and truth are resting on what God has proclaimed in the Scriptures. Any teaching not supported in the Bible is not of God. May you know in your heart and mind that you are not one of the deceived and may you, with all your heart, show your love for God by loving His Living Word. And finally, may you press on towards the upward call of God and be found ready—for there will indeed be *a time of departing!*

> **For false christs and false prophets will rise and show great signs and miracles to deceive, if possible, even the elect. See, I have told you beforehand (Matthew 24:24,25).**

GLOSSARY

Ancient Wisdom

The supposed laws of the Universe that, when mastered, enable one to control one's own reality—another word for metaphysics or occultism.

Aquarius/Aquarian Age

Sign of the Zodiac represented by the water carrier, Earth Age associated with this astrological sign. The term New Age refers to the coming Aquarian age which is in the process of replacing the Pisces age. According to astrologers, every 2,000 years constitutes an age. New Agers predict this Aquarian age will be a time of utopia.

Alice Bailey

British-born occultist who wrote under the guidance of a familiar spirit and channeled nineteen books on the New Age. She also popularized the term.

Centering/Centering Prayer

Another term for meditation (going deep within your center). A type of meditation being promoted in many mainline churches under the guise of *prayer.*

Chakras

Believed by New Agers to be the seven energy centers in man which open up during the kundalini effect in meditation.

Christ-Consciousness

Taught by New Agers to be the state of awareness, reached in meditation, in which one realizes that one is divine and one with God and thereby becoming a Christ or an enlightened being.

Contemplative Prayer

Going beyond thought by the use of repeated prayer words.

Creative Visualization

Imaging in the mind, during meditation, what you want to occur and then expecting it to happen. In simple terms, you are creating your own reality.

Desert Fathers

Mystics who first taught the practice of contemplative prayer.

False Self

The *false self* is the ego or personality that is observable by others. One rids oneself of the false self to find the *true self* through mantra-meditation. New Agers would consider people like Buddha, Ghandi, and even Jesus Christ as examples of people who found their true self.

Guru

Master of Metaphysics who teaches students how to attain their optimal spiritual level.

Higher Self

Supposed God Self within that New Agers seek to connect with through meditation. Also called the Christ Self.

Kundalini

Powerful energy that is brought on through meditation, associated with the Chakras.

Mantra

Word or words repeated either silently or verbally to induce an altered state.

Meditation

Meditation is practiced by all major world religions and is often described as an essential discipline for spiritual growth. Yet, like mysticism, there is great diversity in the practice of meditation. While some see mediation as simply spending time thinking quietly about life or about God, others use meditation techniques to experience altered states of consciousness that allow them to have esoteric experiences. In addition, meditation is promoted in secular society for the personal benefits of health, relaxation and improved productivity.

New Age

The Age of Aquarius, supposedly the Golden Age, when man becomes aware of his power and divinity.

New Thought

Movement that tries to merge classic occult concepts with Christian terminology.

Occult/Occultism

Kept secret or hidden; the practice of metaphysics throughout history.

Pantheism

God *is* all things. The universe and all life are connected in a sum. This sum is the total reality of God. Thus, man, animals, plants, and all physical matter are seen as equal. The assumption—all is one, therefore all is deity.

Panentheism

God is *in* all things. In panentheism God is both personal and is also in all of creation. It is a universal view that believes God is in all people and that someday all of God's creation will be saved and be one with Him.

Reiki

Spiritual energy that is channeled by one attuned to the Reiki power. Literally translated God energy.

Self-Realization

Full contact with the higher self resulting in *knowing* one's self to be *God.*

Theosophical Society

Organization founded by Helena P. Blavatsky in 1875, to spread the Ancient Wisdom (i.e. occultism) throughout Western society. The forerunner of the modern New Age movement.

The silence

Absence of normal thought.

Universalism

All humanity has or will ultimately have a positive connection and relationship with God.

ENDNOTES

FOREWORD

1. Francis Schaeffer, *The God Who Is There*, InterVarsity Press, Downers Grove, Illinois, 1968, p. 66.
2. William Gurnall, *The Christian in Complete Armor*, Moody Press, Chicago, Illinois, 1994, Dec. 13th reading.

1 The Invisible Denomination

1. David Spangler, *Emergence, the Rebirth of the Sacred*, Dell Publishing Co., New York, NY, 1984, p.26.
2. Michael D. Antonio, *Heaven on Earth*, Crown Publishing, New York, N.Y., 1992, p.13.
3. Robert C. Fuller, *Spiritual But Not Religious*, Oxford University Press Inc., N.Y., 2001, p.99
4. "The Guiding Light," *Sales and Marketing Management* magazine August 1997, p.48.
5. *The Reiki News*, Fall 1997, p.16D.
6. "Evolving Boundaries," *Common Boundary* magazine, Jan./Feb., 1994, p.5.
7. "You Gotta Have Faith," *TV Guide Magazine*, March 29, 1997, p.36.
8. Marion Weinstein, *Positive Magic: Occult Self-Help*, Phoenix Publishing, Custer, Washington, 1978. p.19.
9. Ibid, p.25.
10. Mark B. Woodhouse, *Paradigm Wars, World Views for a New Age*, Frog Ltd. Publishing, 1996, p.47.
11. Richard Kirby, *The Mission of Mysticism*, The Camelot Press, Ltd., 1979, p.6.

12. Ann Wise, *The High Performance Mind*, Tarcher/Putnam, Los Angeles, CA., 1995, p.57.

13. Barry Long, *Meditation, a Foundation Course*, Barry Long Books, 1995, p.13.

14. Swami Rama, *Freedom From the Bondage of Karma*, Himalayan Institute, 1977, p.66.

15. Louann Stahl, *A Most Surprising Song*, Unity Books, Unity Village, Missouri, 1992, pp.147-148.

16. W.E. Butler, *Lords of Light*, Destiny Books, Rochester, Vermont, 1990, p.74.

17. David L. Smith, *A Handbook of Contemporary Theology*, Victor Books, 1992, p.273.

18. Brian Tracy, *Maximum Achievement*, Simon and Schuster, New York, N.Y., 1993, pp.179, 17.

19. "Change of Heart," *The Sunday Oregonian*, September 19, 1993, p. L 1.

20. *AM Northwest Morning Talk Show*, KATU Channel 2, Portland, OR, Interview with Wayne Dyer, March 27, 1997.

21. "Living with Vision," *Science of Mind*, April 1, 1992, p.44.

22. Shakti Gawain, *Creative Visualization*, Nataraj Publishing Novato, CA, 2002, back cover.

23. Shakti Gawain, *Creative Visualization*, Nataraj Publishing Novato, CA, 9th Printing, 1983, p.57

24. Julie Cameron, *The Artist's Way*, William Morrow Co., New York, N.Y., 10th Anniversary Edition, front cover, back cover.

25. *What's New at Stiles* newsletter, 1985

26. Terry Mattingly, "Marketplace of the Gods," *Christian Research Journal*, May/June 1986, p.6.

27. *Omega Center for Holistic Studies* Catalog, 1999, p.14.

28. "The New Spirituality," *Maclean's magazine*, Oct. 10, 1994, p.45.

29. "Searching for the Soul," *Newsweek Magazine*, Nov. 28, 1994, p.54.

30. George Trevelyan, *A Vision of the Aquarian Age*, Stillpoint

Publishing, Walpole, New Hampshire, 1984, p. 161.

31. W.E. Butler, *Lords of Light*, op. cit., p.164.

32. Storma Swanson, *Attuning to Inner Guidance*, Seabreeze Press, Beaverton, Oregon, 1982.

33. Jacqueline Small, *Embodying Spirit*, Harper Collins Publishers, New York, NY, 1994, p.97.

34. Geoffrey Parrinder, *World Religions from Ancient History to the Present*, Facts on File Publications, New York, N.Y., 1971, p.155.

35. Rev. Leddy Hammock, *Questions, Answers, and Ultimate Answers* pamphlet, Unity-Clearwater Church, Clearwater, Florida

36. "Kundalini Demystified," *Yoga Journal*, Issue 64, September/October 1985, p.43.

37. "Baba Beleaguered," *Yoga Journal*, Issue 63, July/August 1985, p.30 (reprinted from Co-Evolution Quarterly).

38. Ibid, p.30.

2 The Yoga of the West

1. William Johnston, *Letters to Contemplatives*, Orbus Books, 1992, p.1.

2. Alice Bailey, *From Intellect to Intuition*, Lucis Publishing Co., New York, NY, 1987, 13th printing, p.193.

3. William Johnston, *Lord, Teach Us to Pray*, Harper Collins Publishers, New York, NY, 1991. p.54

4. Ibid, p.58.

5. Walter A. Elwel, *Evangelical Dictionary of Theology*, Baker Book House, Grand Rapids, MI, 1984, p. 818.

6. Fr. Ken Kaisch, *Finding God: A Handbook of Christian Meditation*, Paulist Press, New York, N.Y., 1994, p.283.

7. William Johnson, *The Mystical Way*, Harper Collins, New York, NY, 1993, p.224.

8. Willigis Jager, *Contemplation: A Christian Path*, Triumph Books, Ligouri, MO, 1994, p.93.

9. Richard Kirby, *The Mission of Mysticism*, op. cit., p.7

10. William Johnston, *Letters to Contemplatives*, op. cit., p.13.

11. Willigis Jager, *Contemplation: A Christian Path*, Triumph Books, 1994, p.31.

12. Fr. Ken Kaisch, *Finding God*, op. cit., quoted, from The Cloud of Unknowing, p. 223.

13. "Talking to God," *Newsweek Magazine*, January 6, 1992, p.44.

14. Michael Leach, *America*, May 2, 1992, p.384.

15. M. Basil Pennington, *Centered Living: The Way of Centering Prayer*, Doubleday Publishing, 1988, p.10.

16. Sheed & Ward Catalog, Winter/Lent, 1978, p.12.

17. William Shannon, *Seeds of Peace*, Crossroad, 1996, p.25.

18. "Resting in God," *Common Boundary* magazine, Sept./Oct. 1997, p.25.

19. *Catechism of the Catholic Church*, Urbi et Orbi Communications., 1994, p.652.

20. Randy England, *The Unicorn in the Sanctuary*, Trinity Communications, 1990, p.159.

21. "Get Thee to a Monastery," *Publisher's Weekly*, April 10, 2000, p.39.

22. Bruce Epperly, *Crystal & Cross*, Twenty-third Publishers, Mystic, CT, 1996, p.14.

23. William Shannon, *Seeds of Peace*, op. cit., p.66.

24. Daniel Goleman, *The Meditative Mind*, Tarcher/Putnam Inc., Los Angeles, CA, 1988, p.53.

25. Fr. Ken Kaisch, *Finding God*, op. cit., p.191.

26. Father William Teska, *Meditation in Christianity*, Himalayan Institute., 1973, p.65.

27. Tilden Edwards, *Living in the Presence*, Harper & Row, San Francisco, CA, 1987, Acknowledgement page.

28. Jacquelyn Small, *Awakening in Time*, Bantam Books, New York, N.Y., 1991, p.261.

29. Ronald S. Miller, Editor of *New Age Journal*, *As Above So Below*, Tarcher/Putnam Los Angeles, CA, 1992, p.52.

30. Tav Sparks, *The Wide Open Door,* Center City, MN, Hazelden Educational Material, 1993, p.89.

31. Tilden Edwards, *Spiritual Friend,* Paulist Press, New York, 1980, pp.162-163.

32. Ibid, p.18.

33. Charles Spurgeon, *Morning and Evening,* Hendrickson Publishers, 1991, p.392.

34. Philip St. Romain, *Kundalini Energy and Christian Spiritual ity,* Crossroad Pub. Co., 1995, p.24

35. Ibid., pp.20-21.

36. Ibid., pp.22-23.

37. Ibid., pp.28-29.

38. Ibid., p.107.

39. Ibid., pp.48-49.

40. Ibid., p.39.

41. Ibid., pp.75-76

42. Deborah Hughes and Jane Robertson-Boudreaux, *Metaphysical Primer,* Metagnosis Pub., 1991, p.27.

43. St. Romain, *Kundalini Energy and Christian Spirituality,* op. cit., p.107.

44. Willigis Jager, *Contemplation: A Christian Path,* op. cit., p.72.

45. Michael J. Gelb, *The How to Think Like Leonardo da Vinci Workbook,* Dell Publishing, New York, N.Y., 1999, p.142.

46. John F. MacArthur, *Reckless Faith,* Crossway Books, 1994, p.154-155.

47. "Are You Religious or Are You Spiritual?," *Spirituality & Health Magazine,* Spring 2001, p.28

3 Proponents and Visionaries

1. Michael Tobias, *A Parliament of Souls in Search of a Global Spirituality,* KQED Inc., San Francisco, CA, 1995, p.148.

2. Marilyn Ferguson, *The Aquarian Conspiracy,* J.P. Tarcher Inc., Los Angeles, CA, 1980, p.419.

3. *Life magazine,* December 1992, p.73.

4. *Wall Street Journal*, as quoted in *The Road Less Traveled Seminar*, brochure presented by Career Track, 1992. p.7.

5. M. Scott Peck, *The Road Less Traveled*, Simon & Schuster, Inc., New York, N.Y., 1978, p.283.

6. Ibid, p.309.

7. *New Age Journal*, December 1985, pp.28-30.

8. M. Scott Peck, *A World Waiting to be Born*, Bantam Books, New York, N.Y., 1993, p.88.

9. Ibid., p.21

10. Ibid, p.21

11. Ibid, p.83.

12. Ibid, back cover.

13. Matthew Fox, *The Coming of the Cosmic Christ*, Harper & Row Pub., San Francisco, CA, 1988, pp. 154, 232.

14. Ibid, back cover.

15. Ibid

16. M. Scott Peck, *Further Along the Road Less Traveled*, Simon & Schuster Audioworks, 1992.

17. Ibid

18. Ibid

19. Ibid

20. Ibid

21. Ibid

22. Ibid

23. Michael D. Antonio, *Heaven on Earth*, Crown Publishing, New York, 1992, p.342, 352.

24. Thomas Merton, *Conjectures of a Guilty Bystander*, Doubleday, Garden City, New York, 1989, pp.157-158.

25. *Borders Books for the Nineties* catalog, Fall, 1995, p.15.

26. *Credence Cassettes* magazine, Winter/Lent, 1996, p.59.

27. *Credence Cassettes* magazine, Winter/Lent, 1998, p.24

28. M. Basil Pennington, *Thomas Merton, My Brother*, New City Press, Hyde Park, New York, 1996, p.115. (Quoted from *The Hidden Ground of Love*, pp.63-64.)

29. Nevill Drury, *The Dictionary of Mysticism and the Occult*, Harper & Row Publis, San Francisco, 1985, p. 85.

30. Shirley MacLaine, *Going Within: A Guide for Inner Transformation*, Bantam Books, New York, N.Y., 1989, p. 74.

31. William Shannon, *Silent Lamp, The Thomas Merton Story*, Cross-road Pub. Co., New York, N.Y., 1992, p. 276.

32. Ibid., p. 281.

33. Ibid, p. 273.

34. Deba P. Patnaik, *The Message of Thomas Merton*, edit. Brother Patrick Hart, Cistercian Publishing, Kalamazoo, MI, 1981, p. 87.

35. Michael Ford, *Wounded Prophet: A Portrait of Henri J.M. Nouwen*, Doubleday, Pub., New York, 1999, p. 35.

36. Henri Nouwen, *Sabbatical Journey*, Crossroad Publish ing Co., New York, 1998, p.51.

37. Eknath Easwaran, *Meditation*, Nilgiri Press, Tomoles, CA, back cover, 1991 edition.

38. Thomas Ryan, *Disciplines for Christian Living*, Paulist Press, Mawah, N.J., 1993, pp. 2-3.

39. Henri Nouwen, *The Way of the Heart*, Harper, San Francisco, 1991, p.81.

40. Henri Nouwen, *Bread for the Journey*, Harper, San Francisco, 1997, Jan. 15 and Nov. 16.

41. Henri Nouwen, *The Way of the Heart*, op. cit. p. 66.

42. M. Basil Pennington, Thomas Keating, Thomas E. Clarke, *Finding Grace at the Center*, St. Bede's Pub., Petersham, MA, 1978, pp. 5-6.

43. Thomas Keating, *Intimacy with God*, Crossroad Pub., New York, N.Y., 1994, p. 153.

44. "Talking to God," *Newsweek magazine*, Jan. 6, 1992, p. 44.

45. Gerald May, *Simply Sane*, Paulist Press, Ramsey, N.J., 1977, p. "In Appreciation."

46. Gerald May, *Addiction and Grace*, Harper, San Francisco, CA, Paperback edition, p. 102.

47. Ibid, p. 166.
48. Gerald May, *The Awakened Heart*, Harper, San Francisco, 1991, p. 179.
49. Ibid, p. 179-180.
50. "In the Spirit of the Early Christians," *Common Boundary* magazine, Jan./Feb. 1992, p. 19.
51. Ibid
52. "Lives of the Heart and Soul," *Maclean's* magazine, Sept. 14, 1987, p. 42.

4 *Evangelical Hybrids*

1. Richard Foster, *Celebration of Discipline*, Harper & Row Pub., San Francisco, CA, 1978 edition, p. 13.
2. *Renovare Conference* brochure, Oct. 15-16, 1999, Lynden, WA.
3. *Renovare Conference* brochure, Sept. 13-14, 1996, Fuller Theological Seminary.
4. Richard Foster, *Prayer: Finding the Heart's True Home*, Harper, San Francisco, 1992, p.160.
5. M. Basil Pennington, *Centered Living, The Way of Centering Prayer*, Doubleday Pub., New York, N.Y., 1986 and 1988 editions, p. 104.
6. Matthew Fox, *The Coming of the Cosmic Christ*, Harper & Row Pub., San Francisco, CA, 1988, p. 123.
7. Timothy Freke, *The Spiritual Canticle, the Wisdom of the Christian Mystics*, Godsfield Press, 1998, p. 60.
8. Willigis Jager, *The Search for the Meaning of Life*, Ligouri, MO, 1995, p. 125.
9. Richard Foster, *Prayer: Finding the Heart's True Home*, op. cit. p.122.
10. Richard Foster, *Celebration of Discipline*, 1978 Edition, op. cit. p. 15.
11. Richard Foster, *Prayer: Finding the Heart's True Home*, op. cit., p.124

12. Anthony de Mello, *Sadhana: A Way to God*, St. Louis, the Institute of Jesuit Resources, 1978, p. 28.

13. Richard Foster, *Renovare Conference*, Salem, OR, Nov. 1994.

14. Richard Foster, *Renovare Conference*, op. cit.

15. David Steindl-Rast, "Recollection of Thomas Merton's Last Days in the West," Monastic Studies, 7:10, 1969.

16. Raymond Bailey, *Thomas Merton on Mysticism*, Image Books, 1987, p. 191.

17. Richard Foster and Emilie Griffen, *Spiritual Classics*, Harper, San Francisco, CA, 2000, p. 17.

18. Richard Foster, *Meditative Prayer*, InterVarsity Christian Fellowship, 1983.

19. Richard Foster and James Bryan Smith, *Devotional Classics*, Harper, San Francisco, CA, 1990, 1991, 1993, p. 61.

20. Ibid.

21. Brother Patrick Hart-Editor, *The Message of Thomas Merton*, Cistercian Publications, Kalamazoo, MI, 1981, p. 63.

22. Rosemary Ellen Guiley, *The Miracle of Prayer*, Pocket Books, 1995, p. 227.

23. Richard Foster, *Celebration of Discipline*, Revised Edition 1988, p. 103.

24. Ibid, p. 7.

25. "Book of the Year Reader's Poll", *Christianity Today*, April 5, 1993, p. 26.

26. Ibid, p. 27.

27. Brennan Manning, *The Signature of Jesus*, Multnomah Books, Sisters, OR, 1996, p. 209.

28. Ibid, p. 212.

29. Brennan Manning, *The Ragamuffin Gospel*, Multnomah Press, Sisters, OR, 1990, p. 224.

30. Brennan Manning, *Reflections for Ragamuffins*, Harper, San Francisco, CA, 1998, back cover.

31. Brennan Manning, *The Signature of Jesus*, op. cit., p. 211.

32. *Credence Cassettes*, Winter/Lent 1985 Catalog, p.14.

33. Ibid

34. Tilden Edwards, *Spiritual Friend*, Paulist Press, N.Y., 1980, p.18.

35. "Living as God's Beloved," *Discipleship Journal*, Issue 100, 1997, p.78.

36. William Shannon, *Silence on Fire*, The Crossroad Pub., 1995, p.160.

37. Rodney R. Romney, *Journey to Inner Space*, Riverview Press, New York, N.Y., 1986, p.132.

38. Ibid, p. 138.

39. Ken Carey, *The Starseed Transmissions*, A Uni-Sun Book, 1985 4th printing, p.33.

40. Brennan Manning, *The Signature of Jesus*, op. cit., p. 212.

41. Ibid, p. 216.

42. Ibid, p. 218.

43. Ibid, p. 215.

44. Brother Patrick Hart-Editor, *The Message of Thomas Merton*, Cistercian Publications, Kalamazoo, MI, 1981, p. 200.

5 Discernment

1. Jack Canfield, Mark Victor Hansen, *Dare to Win*, Berkeley Books, New York, 1994, p. 195.

2. Arielle Ford, *Hot Chocolate for the Mystical Soul*, Penguin Putnam Inc., New York, N.Y., 1998, pp. 244-247, 361

3. Ibid, p. 36-39.

4. Ibid, p. 15.

5. Ibid, pp. xiii-xiv.

6. Ibid, back cover.

7. Peggy J. Jenkins, *Nurturing Spirituality in Children*, Beyond Words Pub., Hillsboro, OR, 1995, p. 129.

8. Ibid, pp. 55, 126.

9. Ibid, front cover.

10. *Omega Center Catalogue*, Omega Institute, Rhinebeck, N.Y., 1999, p.107.

11. Sara Ban Breathnach, *Simple Abundance, A Daybook of Comfort and Joy*, Warner Books, NY, 1995, October 31.

12. "Healing Hands," *New Woman Magazine*, March, 1986, p. 78.

13. William Rand, *Reiki: The Healing Touch*, Vision Pub., Southfield, MI, 1991, p.48.

14. Diane Stein, *Essential Reiki*, The Crossing Press, Inc., Freedom, CA, 1995, p.107.

15. *Reiki News*, Spring 1998, p.4.

16. *Reiki News*, Winter, 1998, p.5.

17. Janeanne Narrin, *One Degree Beyond: A Reiki Journey into Energy Medicine*, Little White Buffalo Pub., Seattle, WA, 1998, p. xviii.

18. Brian C. Taylor, *Setting the Gospel Free*, Continuum Publishing Co., New York, N.Y., 1996, p.76.

19. *USA Weekend* Sunday Supplement, July 24-26, 1987, p. 12.

20. Interview with John Randolph Price, *Science of Mind* magazine, August 1989, p. 24.

21. Joan Borysenko, *Fire in the Soul*, Warner Books, New York, N.Y., 1993, p. 165.

22. Ann Wise, *The High Performance Mind*, J. Tarcher Pub., Los Angeles, LA, 1995, pp. 185-186.

23. "OM is Where the Heart Is," *Newsweek* magazine, Feb. 3, 1992, p. 71.

24. "Yoga's Wider Reach," *USA Weekend* Supplement, March 27-29, 1998, p. 12.

25. "Healer of Hearts" *Newsweek* magazine, March 16, 1998, p. 50.

26. Dr. Dean Ornish, *Dr. Dean Ornish's Program for Reversing Heart Disease*, Ballantine Books, New York, N.Y., 1991, p.247.

27. "Yoga's Wider Reach," op. cit. p. 12.

28. Thomas Ryan, *Prayer of Heart and Body*, Paulist Press, New York, 1995, p.131.

29. Eric Butterworth, *Discover The Power Within You*, Front Cover excerpt by Oprah Winfrey, Harper Row San Francisco, CA.

30. Gary Zukav, *The Seat of the Soul*, Simon & Schuster, New York, 1990, Fireside Edition, p.239.

31. David Spangler, "The New Age is Here," *New Thought* magazine, Spring 1989, p.6.

32. Neil T. Anderson, Terry E. Zuehlke, Julianne S. Zuehlke, *Christ Centered Therapy: The Practical Integration of Theology and Psychology*, Zondervan Publishing House, Grand Rapids, Michigan, 2000, p.61.

6 Could This Really Be the End of the Age?

1. Harold Belyoz, *Three Remarkable Women*, Altai Pub., Flagstaff, Arizona, 1986, p. 207.

2. Ibid, p. 210.

3. Ibid, p. 217.

4. Simons Roof, *About the Aquarian Age*, The Mountain School of Esoteric Studies, 1971, p. 7.

5. John Davis and Naomi Rice, *Messiah and the Second Coming*, Coptic Press, Wyoming, MI, 1982, p. 150.

6. James S. Gordon, *The Golden Guru, The Strange Journey of Bhagwan Shree Rajneesh*, The Stephen Green Press, Lexington, MA, 1987, pp. 235-236.

7. Alice Bailey, *The Reappearance of the Christ*, Lucis Pub. Co., New York, N.Y., 4th Printing, 1962, p.124.

8. "Sri Chimney Lifts Over 7,000 lbs. with One Arm," *Life Times* magazine, Vol. 1, Number 3, p. 45.

9. Marjorie L. Rand, "Healing: A Gift That Awakens," *The Whole Person* magazine, June 1988, p. 40.

10. Davis and Rice, *Messiah and the Second Coming*, op. cit., p. 49.

11. John White, "Jesus, Evolution and the Future of Humanity," *Science of Mind* magazine, Oct. 1981, pp. 40-42.

12. Donald H. Yott, *Man and Metaphysics*, Samuel Weiser, New York, N.Y., 1980, p. 73.

13. Armand Biteaux, *The New Consciousness*, Oliver Press, 1975, p. 128.

14. John Randolph Price, *The Planetary Commission*, Quartus Books, Austin, TX, 1984, pp. 143, 145.

15. John R. Yungblut, *Rediscovering the Christ*, Element Inc., Rockport, Maine, 1991, p. 164.

16. Willigis Jager, *Contemplation: A Christian Path*, Triumph Books, Liguori, Missouri, 1994, pp. 93-94.

17. Rabbi David A. Cooper, *God Is A Verb*, Riverhead Books, New York, 1997, p.1.

18. Alice Bailey, *Problems of Humanity*, Lucis Pub. Co., New York, N.Y., 1993, p.152.

19. Alice Bailey, *The Externalization of the Hierarchy*, Lucis Pub. Co., New York, N.Y., 1976, p. 510.

20. Alice Bailey, *Problems of Humanity*, Lucis Publishing Co., New York, 1993, p.152.

21. A Source Book for Earth's Community of Religions handbook, *What Unites Us?*, Conexus Press, Grand Rapids, MI, 1995, p. 151.

22. Ibid, p. 302.

23. M. Basil Pennington, *Centered Living*, Image Books, New York, N.Y., 1988, p. 192.

24. Tilden Edwards, *Spiritual Friend*, Paulist Press, New York, N.Y., 1980, p. 172.

25. "Catholics Urged To Appreciate Other Faiths," *The Catholic Sentinel*, May 24, 2002, p.3.

26. Richard Kirby, *The Mission of Mysticism*, SPCK Pub., London, 1979, p. 85.

27. Reynolds R. Ekstrom, *New Concise Catholic Dictionary*, Twenty-third Pulications/Bayard, Mystic, CT, 1995.

28. "Rethinking Missions in India," *America*, Nov. 12, 2001, p.12

29. Ibid, p.13.

30. Ibid, p.12.

31. John Gray, *How to Get What You Want and Want What You Have*, Harper Collins Pub., New York, N.Y., 1999, pp. 97-98.

7 Seducing Spirits

1. *Lou Davies Radio Program*, Interview with Richard Foster, Nov. 24, 1998, KPAM radio, Portland, Oregon.

2. Thomas Merton, *Contemplative Prayer*, New York Image Books, Doubleday Pub., 1989, pp. 115-116.

3. Dr. Paul Bubna, President Briefings, C&MA, *Purveyors of Grace or Ungrace*, March 1978.

4. Richard Foster, *Celebration of Discipline*, Harper, San Francisco, CA., 1988, p.19.

5. John R. Yungblut, *Rediscovering the Christ*, Element Books, Rockport, MA, 1991, p. 142.

6. Richard Foster, *Celebration of Discipline*, Harper, San Francisco, CA., 1988, p.20.

7. Sue Monk Kidd, *When the Heart Waits*, Harper, San Francisco, CA, 1990, pp. 47-48.

8. Sue Monk Kidd, *God's Joyful Surprise*, Harper, San Francisco, CA, 1987, p. 55.

9. Ibid, p. 56.

10. Ibid, p. 198.

11. Ibid, pp. 233, 228.

12. Ibid, pp. 228-229.

13. The Ganges is a famous river in India, thought to have holy powers but is actually very polluted.

14. Ursula Burton and Janlee Dolley, *Christian Evolution*, Turnstone Press Ltd., Wellingborough, Northamptonshire, Great Britain, 1984, p. 101.

15. M. Basil Pennington, *Thomas Merton, My Brother*, New City Press, Hyde Park, NY, 1996, pp. 199-200.

16. Lewis Sperry Chafer, *Grace, the Glorious Theme*, Zondervan Publishing, Grand Rapids, MI, 1977 Edition, pp. 313-314.

17. Richard Foster, *Streams of Living Water*, Harper, San Francisco, CA, 1998, p. 273.

18. Ibid, p. 274.

19. *Credence Communications Catalog*, Gift Ideas Edition

20. Ibid.

21. Ibid.

22. Frank X. Tuoti, *The Dawn of the Mystical Age*, Crossroad Publishing Co., New York, N.Y., 1997, p. 127.

23. Brennan Manning, *Abba's Child*, NavPress, Colorado Springs, CO. 1994, p. 180.

24. "Ancient Future Youth Ministry", *Group Magazine*, July/August 1999, pp. 33-34.

25. Ibid, p. 39.

26. Ibid, p. 39.

27. Ibid, p. 39

28. San Francisco Theological Seminary, Lloyd Center Pastoral Counseling Service/Youth Ministry and Spirituality Project, Graduate Theological Union, 3/27/00, Project Directors: Mike Yaconelli and Andrew Dreitcer.

29. Michael Yaconelli, *Dangerous Wonder*, NavPress, Colorado Springs, CO., 1998, p. 16.

30. Henri Nouwen, *In The Name of Jesus*, Crossroad, New York, 1989, p.6, pp. 31-32.

31. Henri Nouwen, *Sabbatical Journey*, Crossroad Publishing Company, New York NY, 1998, p.20.

32. Ibid, p.20.

33. Ibid, p.51.

34. Ibid, p. 20.

35. "Understanding Buddhism: Religion Without God," *Shambhala Sun Magazine*, Reginald A. Ray, July 2001, p.25.

36. Taken from web site of the Reiki Centre in Ontario, Canada

37. David G. Benner, *Sacred Companions: The Gift of Spiritual Friendship & Direction*, InterVarsity Press, Downers Grove, Illinois, 2002, p.9.

Index

J

K

L

M

N

RECOMMENDED BOOKS

THE COMPLETE WORKS OF FRANCIS A. SCHAEFFER
Compiled by Crossway Books
ISBN 0891073310
© 1992

THE COMPROMISED CHURCH
By John Armstrong (Editor)
ISBN 1581340060
© 1998 Crossway Books

DEATH IN THE CITY
By Francis Schaeffer
ISBN 1581344023
©2002 Crossway Books

THE EVANGELICAL DICTIONARY OF THEOLOGY
By Walter A. Elwell
ISBN 0801020751
©1984 Baker Book House

FAR FROM ROME, NEAR TO GOD
The Testimonies of 50 Converted Priests
 By Richard Bennett
ISBN 0851517331
©1998 Banner of Truth

FOR MANY SHALL COME IN MY NAME
By Ray Yungen
ISBN 1879112019
©1991 Solid Rock Books, Inc.

THE GOD WHO IS THERE
By Francis Schaeffer
ISBN 0830819479
©1968 InterVarsity Press

GRACE, THE GLORIOUS THEME
By Lewis Sperry Chafer
ISBN 0310223318
©1965 Zondervan

THE LESS TRAVELED ROAD AND THE BIBLE : A Scriptural
Critique of the Philosophy of M. Scott Peck
by H. Wayne House, Richard Abanes
ASIN: 0889651175
© 1995 Christian Publications

MY UTMOST FOR HIS HIGHEST
By Oswald Chambers

THE NEW AGE MOVEMENT AND THE BIBLICAL WORLDVIEW
by John Newport
ISBN 0802844308
©1998 Wm. B Eerdmans Publishing Co.

PAGANS IN THE PEWS
By Peter Jones
ISBN 0830727981
©2001Regal

PREPARING CATHOLICS FOR ETERNITY
By Mike Gendron (Proclaiming the Gospel)
21st Century Press

172

SEDUCTION OF CHRISTIANITY
By Dave Hunt and T.A. McMahon
ISBN 0890814414
©1985 Harvest House Publishers

TWIST OF FAITH
By Berit Kjos
ISBN 0892213582
©1997 New Leaf Press

SPECIAL NOTE FROM RAY YUNGEN

If after having read this book, you are left wondering about your spiritual relationship with God, remember that knowing Jesus Christ is not merely religion or spirituality but rather a personal relationship with Him.

Romans 10:2 speaks of those who have a "zeal for God but not according to knowledge." Many contemplative writers describe a spiritual despondency they suffer before turning to mystical prayer as a remedy and consequently have an acute sense of spiritual failure that propels them into the waiting arms of *the silence*. In contrast the gospel presents a plan that is uniquely initiated by God.

May I first suggest obtaining a copy of Lewis Sperry Chafer's monumental work, *Grace The Glorious Theme*. I have found no other book, which so succinctly and scripturally lays out the Christian faith.

Scripture clearly states that salvation depends entirely on the grace of God: "For by grace you have been saved through faith, and that not of yourselves; it is the gift of God, not of works ..." (Ephesians 2:8,9). Furthermore, Christ's death on the Cross for our sins, fully solidifies in our minds a tangible expression of the unearned and undeserved nature of our salvation. When Jesus said, "It is finished!" (John 19:30), He proclaimed in three words that our salvation depends entirely on the finished work of Christ on the Cross.

Let me therefore caution you in following any teaching that suggests that Christ's work was incomplete or unnecessary, or that there are other paths to God. Christianity is uniquely different from all religions in that it does not contain the erroneous premise that man is basically good (or divine) and consequently can earn his way to Heaven. If you have never found the peace of knowing Christ, I urge you to read the first five chapters of the book of Romans and allow the Holy Spirit to draw you to what is being said and offered. The only prerequisite is to recognize your inability as a sinner to save yourself. Then, in simple faith, tell God you are now trusting Christ, and Him alone, to be your Lord and Savior. "Therefore having been justified by faith, we have peace with God through our Lord Jesus Christ, through whom also we have access by faith into His grace in which we stand ..." (Romans 5:1-2).

To order additional copies of

A TIME
of
DEPARTING

send $12.95* plus $1.50 ($2.50 for priority) for shipping to:

Lighthouse Trails Publishing Company
P.O. Box 958
Silverton, Oregon 97381

**You may also order by calling or faxing our
toll free number: 866/876-3910
[ORDER LINE ONLY]
or emailing editor@lighthousetrails.com .**

For all other calls, call 503/873-9092.

If you would like to order a copy of Mr. Yungen's first book,
For Many Shall Come In My Name,
send $7.95 plus $2.00 for shipping.

* Discount prices for quantity orders of 10 or more.
You may correspond with Ray Yungen at
ray@lighthousetrails.com

Our books may also be ordered through our website
www.lighthousetrails.com